CASES AND APPLICATIONS IN NONPROFIT MANAGEMENT

CASES AND APPLICATIONS IN NONPROFIT MANAGEMENT

EDITED BY

Robert T. Golembiewski
University of Georgia

Jerry G. Stevenson
University of Arkansas at Little Rock

F.E. PEACOCK PUBLISHERS, INC.
Itasca, Illinois

Contents

SECTION 3
Strategies for Managing and Improving Nonprofit, Voluntary, and Third-Sector Organizations

Foreword

As a teacher of graduate nonprofit management courses and as past Chair of the Nonprofit Section in the National Association for Schools of Public Administration and Affairs (NASPAA), I'm repeatedly asked two entirely different sets of questions from colleagues in the public management arena and by management and executive friends in the nonprofit sector.

My public management cohorts query:

- What makes nonprofits any different from the public and/or the for-profit sector when it comes to management?
- Given the increasingly complex relationship between governments and nonprofits, shouldn't the public management literature include that of the nonprofit arena?

Management and executive friends in the nonprofit sector ask:

- Why should we pay attention to management directions, advice, and theories from the public sector, when it may be more essential to "find our way" separate from the "failures" of public and marketplace management tools?
- Given the sheer variety in the nonprofit sector, can any set of management theories, models, and applications really apply to organizations ranging from fairly simple community-based organizations managed by volunteers to complex national human service delivery organizations?

The answer to all four of these questions is most typical for someone who works in the academic arena...**it all depends.**

To the public sector questioners, it depends on the issues of interrelationship and interdependence. In this era of contracting out, privatization, and downsizing in the public sector, some nonprofit organizations are extensions of what was a public sector delivery structure, now moved "out" to the nonprofit arena. Often in such cases, the rules and regulations of that relationship are little more than an extension of the sponsoring public sector organization. At the heart of the issue, however, is the concern from policy makers as to whether the spirit of "contracting out" is lost in such duplication. In these contracting-out environments, the latitude for management structures varies greatly and the nonprofit organization is likely to have multiple sources of funding, possible from public and for-profit arenas simultaneously.

The second question is at the heart of the need for this kind of casebook: what makes the nonprofit arena so "different" that public (or alternatively, for-profit) management cases are not sufficient? After all, many governmental organizations do have governing boards, volunteers involved in service delivery, fiscal diversity including fund-raising, and even some "for-profit" concerns. The key literature on nonprofits about the uniqueness of this sector is quite diverse, but there are two broad components that make it fundamentally "different."

First, the uniqueness of the nonprofit sector is tied to its long history of philanthropic endeavors and its "voluntary" nature. From the work by Andrew Carnegie in the late 1800s to recent examinations of the field, nonprofits derive part of their fundamental "definition" from the view that philanthropy and voluntary associations have their own unique problems, especially in management. Yes, governments "fund-raise" beyond the traditional revenue-generation devices of taxes, but nonprofits are fundamentally defined by the fact that responsibility for revenues involves a complex relationship between society and the organization's own specific mission. Yes, governments require some sort of "approval" by the public, but nonprofits' existence depends on the voluntary nature of relationships.

Second, nonprofits have a special role as a "third sector" either between the two dominant sectors or as a boundary spanner beyond them. Thus, literature on public or private management must define itself fundamentally around its legal and for-profit "core values." But nonprofits must define their role around a more complex conceptualization of mission, sometimes internally defined, sometimes defined by external actors. Although "mission" is a popular term in both of the traditional management arenas currently, it is the defining characteristic of the nonprofit world.

But if such analysis justifies the "special" case of nonprofits, why should nonprofit managers (or those seeking careers in that sector) look to a book of cases edited by two public management scholars? Moreover, can the sheer variety of nonprofits be effectively dealt with in a single casebook?

The ultimate test, of course, is the utility of this volume by academics and practitioners alike. However, the need for such a casebook is clear. Too often, both academics and practitioners have "adjusted" or "adapted" casebooks from the other sectors, or they have been dependent on a small number of practitioners to create special cases in the area. Most of the former efforts have frustrated those of us who teach in this developing arena. As to the latter problem, most of the practitioners tend to concentrate on single issues, especially those of boards, volunteers, and fund-raising.

This is a unique time in the history of nonprofit organizations. While massive "contracting out" is occurring, there is a corresponding attack on nonprofits' tax status from competitors primarily in the for-profit sector. As demands are made for nonprofits to develop alternative delivery structures, the level of accountability for those actions is increasing. While management gurus such as Peter Drucker write volumes on the need for the other two sectors to "copy" the successes of the third sector, writers such as Lester Salamon remind us of the fundamental instability of this much smaller sector.

Yes, it is time for a "nonprofit" casebook. In both the "micro" example of individual cases presented here as well as the fundamental issues addressed previously, the student can develop a better understanding of the complexity of this sector. I began this

Foreword with a set of questions from the public and nonprofit sector. Now, I pose two additional questions for the student:

- From the cases presented here, are the particular problems and conceptual issues of this third sector the kinds of arenas that I find interesting and challenging for my own career?
- Can I learn beyond the "specifics" in these cases to understand the particular issues that must define working in the nonprofit sector?

If the student answers these questions in the affirmative, then he or she should utilize these cases in forming career directions (whether already in process or not!) as well as in coming to a deeper understanding of what it takes to be an effective nonprofit manager. The future of the nonprofit sector will certainly be guided by events in its external and internal environments, but effective management of the arena must be at the helm.

Roby Robertson
Director, Institute of Government
University of Arkansas at Little Rock

Preface

There is a growing need for well-prepared managers of nonprofit organizations. Over the past two decades there has been a tremendous upsurge in organized voluntary activity and the creation of nonprofit or non-governmental organizations. As the nonprofit or third sector continues to grow in importance and in the diversity of professionals in the field, the role of effective management is becoming even more critical. Consequently, it is important that educational and training resources be available that target the specific challenges faced by the nonprofit sector.

In this book we address a broad range of realistic management situations and problems encountered in nonprofit organizations. Features include a substantial introduction explaining how to use cases in the classroom as well as exercises and questions that help students delineate some of the unique issues facing nonprofit managers today. The cases are also organized by major behavioral themes (e.g., strategies for managing and improving nonprofit organizations) as well as by managerial focus and function (e.g., board and staff relations, collaboration, conflict management, ethical dilemmas, human resource management, philanthropy and volunteers).

In Section 1, we introduce the reader to the dynamic context and environment of nonprofit management.

In Section 2, we present the key dimensions of organizing and managing nonprofit organizations.

In Section 3, our focus is on strategies for managing and improving nonprofit organizations.

The Alternative Table of Contents classifies the cases by managerial focus and function to help the instructor target specific cases for various pedagogical strategies.

The collection of cases and applications in this book should be useful to students in courses about nonprofit management both at undergraduate and graduate levels as well as various nonprofit management development training courses. The National Association of Schools of Public Affairs and Administration (NASPAA) recently redefined the "public" in "public administration" to include the nonprofit sector, and the Academy of Management Division for the Public Sector changed its name to the Division for Public and Nonprofit Sectors. Both changes illustrate the increasing attention being directed to the management of nonprofit agencies. Additionally, more and more public and business administration programs offer a specialization in nonprofit management.

We hope that instructors using this book will consider the Introduction an integral part of the text and will find it helpful in preparing their own classroom objectives. Instructors who assign the Introduction to their students and discuss it with them in class will find that their students also benefit.

Several cases have been previously published and are reprinted here with permission, as noted in Cases by Contributor at the back of the book. A grateful acknowledgment is due those whose names appear in Contributors to Series of Casebooks, also at the back of the book. Several individuals who provided cases or other information prefer to remain unidentified. Their contributions are gratefully, if anonymously, acknowledged.

The editors wish to acknowledge the excellent editorial help provided by Janet Tilden as well as the professional clerical assistance given by Amanda Midkiff at the University of Arkansas at Little Rock. We also extend our sincere appreciation to Peggy and Steve, respectively. This manuscript would not have been possible without their continuing love, encouragement, and support.

All cases and applications in this book are abstractions from reality and are primarily a conflation of the experiences of a number of individuals in the same general class. Moreover, numerous inventions seek to highlight type-situations without reference to specific individuals. Any similarities between persons and organizations are hence not only purely coincidental, but false to the synthetic character of each case.

Introduction

In compiling this book, we were reminded of the TV advertisement sponsored by the competitor of the nation's largest auto rental agency. The stick-people featured in that commercial shout in unison, "We're the other guy!"

When most people think about management issues, they focus on business or the public sector. In this book, we turn our attention to the "other guys"—voluntary nonprofits and other not-for-profit organizations, sometimes referred to collectively as the "third sector."

The size and significance of this "third sector" has increased considerably over the last couple of decades, and this trend is likely to continue. Even a substantial collapse of our governmental and for-profit institutions probably would not dampen this growth curve. In fact, one could argue that such a collapse could actually cause the "other guys" to become even more important.

Political thought of all shadings forecasts a growing role for nonprofit, third-sector, and voluntary sector organizations. Liberals and conservatives disagree on many issues, but they concur on several propositions supporting an enlarging role for the "other guy":

- Governments have limitations on what they can do, even when resources are ample, but especially when resources are declining;

- The business sector cannot and should not do it all; indeed, there are many needed roles that business almost certainly will not perform, because they are incompatible with what now passes for the economic and political philosophy associated with the "market model";
- The more closely a market model is followed, the greater the number of people who are likely to "fall between the cracks" and require aid and support as efficiency and market considerations predominate;
- Government will become increasingly incapable of providing for those who "fall between the cracks" because public resources are at least decelerating, if not actually declining.

Hence, it is not surprising that interest in the third sector has been growing exponentially. A journal targeted to change-agents—the *Organization Development Journal*—recently published a special issue about intervening successfully in the third sector. The requests for copies of that issue nearly doubled the usual number of copies published.

How does this volume address the burgeoning interest in voluntary, nonprofit, and third-sector organizations? Four emphases underlie our approach:

- reliance on two broad categories of cases;
- the goal of engaging learning cycles;
- behavioral themes as a mode of organization;
- managerial focus and function as an alternative mode of classification.

LEARNING VIA TWO KINDS OF "CASES"

This volume features a number of "cases" intended to stimulate learning. Most of the cases fit the conventional mold, as represented by the granddaddy of all institutional providers of case studies—the Harvard Case program. The following caveat, which is printed in various forms on the face of all Harvard Cases (Glover and Hower, 1963, p. 1), neatly sums up both the intent and content of this useful learning aid:

The cases…have been chosen solely on the basis of their intrinsic interest for purposes of discussion. The various points of view and the specific administrative actions set forth are not necessarily intended to represent either correct or incorrect, desirable or undesirable administrative philosophy or behavior.

In effect, cases help the reader to isolate the right questions that require attention, rather than to provide correct answers. Cases expose learners to a broad range of situations they are likely to encounter on the job, allowing them to experiment with different approaches without facing the risks inherent in real-life situations.

We have also included a second category of "cases" or applications that do not fit the conventional mold. Rather than describing action-sequences in a hypothetical situation, these "cases" comprise policy fragments or bits of knowledge designed to evoke useful responses from the learner. In this sense, "case" refers to a probe or stimulus that encourages the reader to take a position, then informs the reader about approaches or "designs" that will aid him or her in being reflexive about that position-taking.

The inquiring case-user might ask: What are the consequences of taking a particular position? Are alternative positions possible, which permits a search for a better balance of attractive versus unattractive consequences? Does a particular position seem based on inconsistent or even contradictory objectives? Fine-tuning follows, and a higher-order synthesis of knowledge may result from such exploration.

ENGAGING LEARNING CYCLES

The rationale for our reliance on cases has two major components. First, experience is an excellent teacher, but it need not always be one's own direct experience. All managerial situations are unique, but certain types of situations tend to recur on a regular basis.

Second, case studies have the capacity to engage learning cycles. What does this mean? Cases can motivate learners to test their inventory of knowledge and values in the context of specific organizational action-sequences that can be related to the past

Figure 1.   The basic learning cycle.

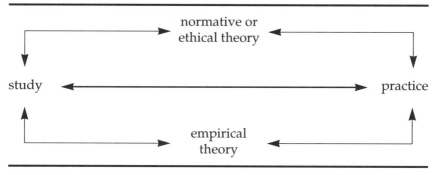

as well as to the future. Broadly, this engagement can be labeled "experiential" or "reflexive," as described below.

1. Basic Learning Cycle. The middle section of Figure 1 highlights the basic learning cycle: study should inform practice, and vice versa. This two-way linkage is schematized as *study ↔ practice.* Ideally, the reflexive manager bounces back and forth between the two, relying on effective study to inform practice, and responding to practical urgencies that motivate study. This approach applies to formal research as well as to developing "job smarts."

To add some perspective relevant to this basic *study ↔ practice* recycling, two kinds of theories are tested and evaluated. To begin, there is "empirical theory"—our attempts to make sense of what goes on around us. A manager or administrator needs a workable empirical theory that is also amenable to continual upgrading.

Of equal significance is one's normative or ethical theory, or philosophy of life. Without it, even the most powerful manager will be an unguided missile. In normative theory, the focus is on what should be done, as well as why. Normative theory derives from multiple sources: professional standards, values, religious beliefs, personal feelings, and so on. Case studies provide convenient contexts in which these components of ethical or normative theory can surface, and dialogue can help sharpen each learner's view of the strengths and weaknesses of particular elements of his or her normative theory.

Figure 2.   Aspects of the experiential learning cycle
(based on Kolb, 1984).

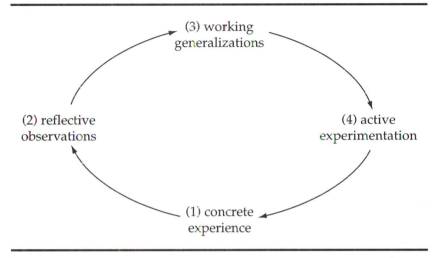

Normative or ethical theory guides the practice of the reflective manager, even as in a critical sense it stands outside that experience. When the manager acts on a particular ethical or normative theory, the action has consequences for the manager as well as for others.

2. Learning and Experience. We can be more specific about how this casebook can help trigger learning based on experience, relying on Kolb's (1984) model. As detailed in Figure 2, an effective learning cycle begins with (1) concrete experience that is subjected to (2) reflective observations by a learner. Over time, the learner fashions increasingly comprehensive frames of reference, or (3) working generalizations, to accommodate this growing store of observations. Through (4) active experimentation, the learner's observations are informed by, as well as tested against, available knowledge and normative perspectives.

SOME BEHAVIORAL TARGETS

The cases in this book can be put to some uses more easily than others, and the Table of Contents provides one set of details for this generalization. In effect, each case tends to raise different issues concerning what we know about human behavior, as well as what we don't know. As a convenience to users, the Table of Contents organizes the cases in terms of their most relevant behavioral themes, selected from the emphases in a major textbook (Rainey, 1997).

Users of this casebook can exploit the Table of Contents in various ways. Behavioral concepts can be used to select the cases most appropriate for each user's purposes, and then a set of readings, or a convenient textbook, may be chosen to provide a detailed context for testing a learner's knowledge and attitudes. Often this kind of testing will enrich the analysis and discussion of specific cases, targeting areas of improvement helpful to specific individuals.

The reader's initial inventory of empirical theory about selected behavioral concepts may be tested against specific cases, as informed by assigned readings. This allows the reader to engage ever-richer learning cycles. Relatedly, the reader's initial normative or ethical theory may be variously tested, extended to fit an enlarged set of action-sequences, or perhaps even discarded on the basis of dialogue with other learners.

MANAGERIAL FOCUS AND FUNCTION AS WAYS TO CLASSIFY CASES

As a more specific way of suggesting how the cases may be used, our Alternative Table of Contents arrays them by managerial focus and function. "Focus" is the more general term referring to major ways of labeling clusters of activities that may be observed in organizations. For example, "diversity" is an important focal lens through which to observe much of what goes on in today's organizations, particularly in the third sector.

Managerial function also can be used to classify the cases and thus to inform readers' judgments about which cases meet their specific needs. These managerial functions fall into two major categories:

- The traditional POSDCORB, or the mnemonic for Planning, Organizing, Staffing, Directing, Coordinating, Reporting, and Budgeting (Waldo, 1948, p. 99).
- Various neologisms such as Human Resources, Information Sciences, and so on. Generally, the two categories of "functions" refer to the same thing: the major clusters of activities that managers and executives perform as they mold institutions and organizations, and as they are molded by them.

Directly, then, the Alternative Table of Contents will help steer readers toward specific cases that are especially relevant to one or more significant clusters of managerial functions. The underlying dual usage of "functions" will help efficiently target the uses to which specific cases can be put in course syllabi, as in associating a specific case with bibliographic items. This cataloging may help readers plan their use of the cases.

PREPARING CASES FOR CLASSROOM AND TRAINING USE

Effective use of the cases in this book requires careful planning. This preparation has two parts: substance and process. *Substance* refers to choosing which issues to emphasize through the *process* techniques chosen. *Process* refers to techniques for using the case in class assignments, group configurations, role-playing, and projective methods.

Preparation of Case Substance

The following is a four-step method for identifying and choosing the issues raised by an individual case. This method allows each instructor (or student) to formulate an individual perspective on the content of a case.

Step One: To analyze the content or substance of a case, read it through a couple of times. As you read, jot down the issues being raised by the characters, situations, and events. The Alternative Table of Contents gives some examples.

Step Two: Compare the issues you have listed with the issues in our list. Peruse the list of issues and see if you want to add to, subtract from, or modify your list. Don't concentrate on how we have classified the case. The purpose of this step is simply to help you consider a full range of issues.

After reviewing the list of issues in the Alternative Table of Contents, you should have a revised list. This will reflect your own experience, education, and personality. There is no "correct" or "incorrect" list—only lists that allow you to use the case with more or less effectiveness for your own course or training objectives.

Step Three: In this step you begin a dialogue with our classifications for the case. Turning to an individual case, compare the list of issues you have prepared in the first two steps with the issues we have checked off for the same case. You may feel comfortable with the differences, or may, after asking yourself "Why have they classified the case in this way?" gain new insight into the possibilities offered by the case. Then make a final list of issues you want to emphasize in class discussion and student assignments.

Step Four: Finally, scan your library and memory as well as the class or training readings. Seek articles, books, or reports that offer pertinent empirical findings, theories, or narratives for the issues you choose to emphasize. Then you will have the substance of the case prepared in some depth. This will help you choose techniques for using the case on the basis of well-thought-out, substantive learning objectives. Once the case has been prepared in this manner, you can easily refresh your preparation from your notes.

Linkages with Selected Readings

Carefully selected readings will enrich and focus the learning potential of cases. They need not be matched one-to-one but can be linked one-to-several or several-to-several. Generally, useful reading assignments are abundantly available in other books and journals and, once an instructor has given some thought to these cases, relevant readings will readily come to mind. The same cases can be used for different purposes with different readings. Although they have been grouped under several topical headings, all are sufficiently rich to allow for alternative topical focus.

We believe that both students and instructors can benefit from the four-step method presented in this section. Instructors might find this method helpful in motivating students to search the relevant journal literature.

Preparation of Cases for Discussion

The number of ways of using cases in the classroom approaches the number of instructors using them. Each instructor has an individual style; each case offers several possibilities; each course or course unit has specific objectives. In preparing a case for classroom use, the instructor must consider his or her objectives and personal style as well as the possibilities offered by the case.

The reader knows more about his or her own style than we know. Do you prefer technical or intuitive approaches? Are you comfortable with conflict among your students or between yourself and the class? Do you like to lead the class toward specific insights or let it grope toward its own discovery? Do you like to create uncertainty and raise questions, or do you have clear and specific course objectives? Each user of this casebook should consider these questions and develop an overall strategy for the use of cases in the context of a specific course and social setting.

Cases themselves constrain their use. Some pose ethical problems; some pose interpersonal problems; some call for the design of behavioral interventions; some demand hard analysis. The instructor must assess the constraints of the case to determine its use. Another dimension imposed is the kind of social arrangements the case permits. Some cases lend themselves to role-playing. Students or trainees can play the characters in the case directly. Several cases emphasize dialogue between characters, while others allow each student to compose a written memorandum, and still others encourage a formal in-class debate.

There are also substantive constraints. For cases involving racial or gender issues, it is particularly important that various

views be represented. Along these lines, some cases have specific legal implications that students might be assigned to explore, such as aspects of tort law.

In general, cases can be planned around a variety of instructional and course objectives, many of which have been noted
earlier in this Introduction. These include (a) indirect socializa-
tion through exposure to real-world experiences in case form;
(b) development of a personal repertoire of responses and behaviors to common but difficult situations that might otherwise
be unknown to the student; (c) developing skills in separating
fact from assumption, and in deducing details from outlines; (d)
practicing the articulation of objectives and the formulation of
strategy in administrative settings involving personal, organizational, and interorganizational relations; (e) experience in
withholding judgment and resisting the temptation to jump to
conclusions before the facts have been assessed and diverse
views heard; (f) improving one's capacity for relating textbook theory to practical settings; (g) experience in group problem analysis
and resolution; (h) improving diagnostic skills and skills at designing effective interventions into administrative settings; (i)
testing one's personal values and objectives; (j) becoming aware
of the values and objectives, strengths and weaknesses of the
specific settings in which one works and lives; (k) acquiring
greater facility at developing and testing the boundaries of behavioral generalizations; (l) relating the "big picture" to the
small instance; (m) learning how to apply traditional concerns in
management and service delivery, such as responsiveness, responsibility, and representativeness, in specific instances—or
how to make the philosophical concrete; (n) encouraging risk-
taking in administrative settings; and (o) becoming personally
aware of the existential dilemmas of nonprofit management.

The individual instructor may have many other objectives in
using these cases in class, and many tactics can facilitate the successful accomplishment of instructional and personal objectives
through case usage. Instructors can provide students with an outline to use while reading cases and, perhaps, ask students to write
each assignment in a standard format. One format, suggested by
Professor Ross Clayton of the University of Southern California,

has a number of variations in common use. The students are requested to respond to the following questions:

- What are the facts available in the case?
- What are the assumptions made in the case?
- What conclusions do you draw from these facts and assumptions?
- What theories, common prescriptions, or legal doctrines are relevant to this case?
- What experiences have you had that come to mind when reading this case, and what have you learned from these experiences that helps you here?
- What recommendations do you make, for whom, and why?

When employing an analytical paradigm of this sort, the students should focus on the concrete rather than on prescriptive generalities such as "follow the steps of a rational decision" or "invite the participation of all concerned."

In a brief article about "process methods" Professor Harold Fox[1] of DePaul University offers a number of practical suggestions about using cases. He asserts that "most classes contain some members who read carelessly, and therefore fail to grasp the point or points of a case." He suggests requesting students to prepare a statement of the objectives of a case, to condense the case into a few carefully chosen words; translate the contents of the case into textbook language and terminology; separate fact from opinion; or prepare a diagram showing the central problems of a case and all the collateral factors associated with it.

Many group-involvement techniques can assist the class in getting the most from a case. Fox suggests the "Phillips 66" technique, in which the class is divided into groups of six, which then have six minutes to form a position and select a leader to present it. The instructor can also hand a class predetermined solutions for a case and invite justification or criticism. A class can be divided into teams for preparation of written or oral reports. An interesting variation on this common classroom technique, im-

---

[1]Harold W. Fox, "Two Dozen Ways of Handling Cases: Depending on How You Count," *Collegiate News and Views* XXVI: 3 (Spring 1973).

plied by Fox, is for the instructor to recommend different ways of dividing the work among different groups. Then the class can observe the consequences of group structure upon each group's decisions. Role-playing in front of the class has been suggested. Several of the cases in this book lend themselves particularly well to this technique, which often involves extending the action beyond the narrative.

The contents can also be altered to gain insight into a case. Fox poses questions such as "What changes in the setting would call for substantial change in the solution?" This alerts case analysts to "sensitivity" questions. Occasionally an instructor may invite managers who have experience dealing with the issues or settings of a case to speak to the class. This can vary classroom pace and add practical insight. Fox also recommends having the class seek analogies to a case situation in current events or in academic writings as a means of "mind stretching."

Fox suggests several techniques to heighten the students' ability to apply insights derived from case analysis. One technique is to ask students to deal with generic situations to which an inventory of probable solutions can be crafted. This technique fosters the development and refinement of principles of action, and the recognition of structural commonalties in managerial situations.

Another technique for promoting the application of case learning is to have the students conduct class or have the students write cases themselves and share them with the class. If this latter technique is chosen, however, it is important to provide the students with guidelines for writing a case. Among the most important: (a) cases should be decision-oriented rather than just descriptive of a situation and contain identifiable issue(s); (b) write the case from the perspective of a specific person, even if that person does not appear directly in the case; and (c) provide sufficient information in the case to use as a basis for making a decision or recommendation.

Each case in this book can be used in several ways. We hope instructors can use the material in this Introduction to encourage creativity in the classroom. We also hope we have made clear the extent to which the cases in this book represent a substantial and flexible pedagogical resource. We welcome constructive advice about the use of the cases, and we hope our suggestions help students and instructors to get the most out of them.

References

Glover, J.D., and Hower, R.M. (Eds.). *The administrator: Cases on human relations in business*. Homewood, IL: Irwin.

Kolb, D. (1984). *Experiential learning*. Englewood Cliffs, NJ: Prentice Hall.

Rainey, H. (1996). *Understanding public organizations* (2nd ed.). San Francisco: Jossey-Bass.

Waldo, D. (1948). *The administrative state*. New York: Ronald Press Company.

Alternative Table of Contents: Classification of Cases by Managerial Focus and Function

Budgeting

Collaboration

Communication

Conflict Management

Training

SECTION 1

The Dynamic Context of Nonprofit, Voluntary, and Third-Sector Organizations

1

Board Membership Has
Its Privileges

Juan is the executive director of Senior Years, an agency whose small staff of three provides various services for the elderly. According to the agency's constitution and bylaws, 75 percent of the agency's board members must be senior citizens. At present, there is one slot open on the board.

At a recent hearing at the state capitol, Juan had a chance to talk with Senator Gonzales, a 67-year-old political veteran who chairs a powerful appropriations committee that handles discretionary funds for programs that serve elderly residents of the state. In addition, he has formed a temporary joint committee to look into allegations of misuse of public monies by agencies that assist the elderly. Juan has been lobbying the senator for additional funds to build a senior center, but he doesn't want to draw undue attention to his agency for fear Gonzales will disapprove of the fact that Juan has regularly used state funds to match federal funds for program delivery. Although this practice is not illegal, Senator Gonzales has made it clear that he considers it inappropriate. In fact, he has stated publicly that any agency caught doing it will be sanctioned and lose state funding.

Juan decides on a plan of action. Tomorrow he will ask his agency's board members to authorize him to invite Senator Gonzales to join the board, figuring that once he is a member, the senator will not only see the value and wisdom of creative fund matching, but will be an even stronger advocate for senior programs in the state. Gonzales has indicated to Juan that he would like to join the board because it will qualify him for reduced rates by his insurance company.

INSTRUCTIONS AND QUESTIONS

1. Is Juan's plan a sound one?
2. What could he possibly gain from his planned strategy? What could he lose?
3. What action should his board take?

2

Friends, Volunteers, and Adversaries: Sorting Out the Players

You are the executive director of a substance abuse treatment and prevention program with a staff of 14, serving 45 residential clients and 150 outpatients and running a comprehensive prevention program in the local schools, with a budget of $850,000. You have served in this capacity for nine years and have built the program from scratch. You are proud of what you and your staff have done. Further, you have relied heavily on the 16 members of the board of directors, 80 percent of whom have been with you since the start.

Recently, however, you have been experiencing some difficulties with a new group of volunteers who have approached you about forming a "Friends of the Program" interest group to assist in fundraising and management of the two residential treatment facilities. You definitely need some help in these areas but are concerned that the well-meaning volunteers may upset the balance you have created among yourself, the staff, and the board.

Among the new "friends" are a state legislator; the spouse of one of your most powerful board members; an outspoken city council member who is unhappy that more drug programs haven't been started in her district; the vice president of the local

Junior League; and four members of the now-defunct Narcotics Anonymous chapter. You recognize the potential strengths that this group could bring to your agency, but you want to assure yourself that their motivations are consistent with what you have been trying to accomplish. You decide to assign your assistant director, Kim, to work directly with this group to help them charter themselves as a "Friends of the Program" group and design projects that will help the agency.

Kim tells you that the group is an aggressive one, full of ideas and eager to help. For example, the state legislator has indicated he will sponsor a bill in the next session to designate your agency as the primary recipient of all block grant funds earmarked for drug treatment in the state. The spouse of the board member has been openly critical of your management style, contending that you spend too much time dealing with funding sources and outside agencies, and too little time in the treatment facilities. The city council member has told you privately that she thinks you're doing a great job but that she must make a public statement about needing more programs in her district so she can get reelected. The Junior Leaguer is a long-time community volunteer who just wants to make a difference. The NA veterans, now drug-free, want to start an "alumni" chapter for those ex-addicts who have stayed clean after treatment in your facilities. Kim tells you that the next meeting of the "Friends of the Program" will be an important one since the group plans to elect officers and decide which project to tackle first.

INSTRUCTIONS AND QUESTIONS

1. You are the executive director. What should you do first?
2. Outline other major priorities.
3. Detail an action plan.

3

Greed, Sex, and Abuse of Power

The *Los Angeles Times* reported that William Aramony, former head of United Way of America (UWA), was convicted of charges that he lived lavishly and romanced women with thousands of dollars of the charity's money. He reportedly spent the money on vacations, luxury apartments, and other items for himself and his teenaged girlfriend. The president of America's largest charity for 22 years, Aramony earned an annual salary of $369,000 plus pension and health care benefits. He is credited with building the UWA into a powerful fund-raising organization, raising $3.2 billion in 1991.

The former UWA director drew a seven-year prison term and was also ordered to repay the nation's largest charity $552,000 for the money he had embezzled. Two of Aramony's top associates were also found guilty of helping him loot UWA and conceal his romances in exchange for first-class travel and other perks. Aramony's former secretary, who had a three-year affair with him, said she used "creative coding" to cover his spending during the seven years she did his expense reports.

News of the scandal led to a dramatic drop in United Way donations, even though each United Way chapter is a separate organization. "Because people did not make the distinction between United Way of America and their local chapters, there were a lot of donors who believed something was wrong with their own United Way," explained Martina Martin, UWA's director of marketing. "Some people canceled pledges, others raised grave concerns. In turn, the only action for some local chapters was to try to distance themselves from UWA, and so they withheld their membership from us."

The nonprofit world has paid close attention to this particular trial. It has created a climate where donors are skeptical. They want to know how an organization is governed and managed financially. In addition, many charity board members are pondering their own potential liability in the event of scandal.

The Aramony scandal also has focused attention on the apparent lack of oversight proved by the board of directors of United Way. The directors discussed UWA business for a few hours each month and then tried to exercise control. "It can't be done," many conclude.

Board membership may increase social status, but it also demands a level of personal responsibility that board members have typically ignored. Both large and small nonprofit boards are typically populated with corporate CEOs, lawyers, and financiers who can read financial reports and know about internal control for their own organizations. Unfortunately, these seasoned business executives seem to lose their capacity for intelligent decision making when it comes to nonprofit boards and certainly do not apply the same standards of care to nonprofits that they apply to running their own businesses.

The legal liability for nonprofit boards could be extensive, except that board members typically receive indemnification from the charity. "There is not much of an incentive to put in the time and effort that is necessary to run the charity effectively," says Daniel Kurtz. "The real problem on boards is getting rid of the deadwood"—that is, directors and board members who are well intentioned but careless, negligent, or inattentive.

Nonprofits are now scrambling to protect themselves. Purchases of liability insurance by charities for their directors and officers have soared since the United Way scandal first broke in 1992. The Aramony case has also fueled a fledgling crusade by some boardroom reformers for term limits for directors. "Board members should serve defined terms, with upper limits on consecutive years of service," asserts William Bowen, president of the Andrew Mellon Foundation and author of *Inside the Board-room: Governance by Directors and Trustees.*

Since the scandal, UWA has restructured its board, adopted new bylaws and created new oversight committees. According to Robert Bothwell, executive director of the National Committee for Responsive Philanthropy, "The monopoly United Way has had for so many years in workplace giving is what produced the unprincipled man that Aramony became." The Aramony scandal, Bothwell concludes, proves that "top-dog arrogance still exists."

INSTRUCTIONS AND QUESTIONS

1. What are the legal liabilities for board members of nonprofits in your state?
2. Do the existing regulations seem adequate to inhibit a UWA-like occurrence? Do you see any major liabilities?
3. How can nonprofits protect themselves from abuses by adminis-trators, especially those who have assembled boards that are "too friendly"?

4

Humanitarian Road to Hell? Some Ravages of International NGO Intervention

Michael Maren recently shocked the reading and giving public with his book *The Road to Hell: The Ravaging Effects of Foreign Aid and International Charity.* Maren's analysis emphasizes six points:

- The number of non-governmental organizations (NGOs) has been increasing rapidly. In the early 1980s, for example, fewer than 150 humanitarian aid agencies were registered with the United States government, and by 1995, the total number had nearly tripled.
- Few people had heard about NGOs even a few years ago, and now they are mentioned constantly by the media; for example, *Doctors Without Borders, Save Our Children,* and other groups have joined old hands such as the *International Committee of the Red Cross* and *Catholic Relief Services* in the popular consciousness.
- On too many occasions, the NGOs have been so numerous at specific sites as to cause problems for each other.
- At times, NGOs have become competitive with one another in the field as they sought funding from private or government sources in home countries.

- At least on some occasions, NGOs have utilized dramatic photos and stories of need to plead their cases for funding, but this zeal has not always been accompanied by efficiency or economy in delivering food or supplies to meet local needs.
- Forecasting needs is a tough business, and some NGOs have (if anything) chosen to publicize high estimates, in part because of poor information but also to encourage a continuous flow of funding.

This list could be extended (Maren, 1997), but its basic character would remain much the same. The "business of foreign aid" by international charities is great and growing, whether the location is Rwanda, Sarajevo, Goma, or wherever. That "business" combines caring with theatrics and at least occasional sleight-of-mind.

For those who want to verify the accuracy of Maren's analysis, critical sources can be consulted (Rieff, 1997).

Exhibit 4-1 lists a number of possible reasons for the rapid proliferation of NGOs in foreign aid.

Exhibit 4-1. Possible Reasons for the Expanding Role of NGOs in Foreign Aid

	Rank Order
NGOs can tell compelling stories via the media, encouraging giving by those who are limited in their ability to check the stories.	_____
People have an absolute right to intervene in extreme cases, and to expect intervention by the more affluent.	_____
Almost anyone can set up an NGO—there are no general requirement for certification, and no regulations exist.	_____
NGOs are "on the ground," and can often supply information to the media, and the media in return can give them good treatment for their fundraising claims, even if exuberant.	_____
The NGO market is big, even huge, with many invaluable sources of funding. Competition among NGOs is inevitable.	_____

It is better to try to solve humanitarian problems even if
political problems remain unsolved.   _____

Specific numbers may attract the bean counters, but good
estimates of need for NGOs are never available until long
after action is necessary. By then, it can be too late.
Hungry or poorly sheltered people will have died.   _____

Humanitarian aid overseas has saved the lives of
hundreds of thousands of people.   _____

Givers are easy to dupe, and the more distant the
problem, the easier they are to fool.   _____

Many people in affluent societies feel guilty about the
poor and disaffected in their own backyards. Giving a
little at a distance replaces doing a lot locally.   _____

Other Possible Reasons	**Rank Orders**
_____	_____
_____	_____
_____	_____
_____	_____

INSTRUCTIONS AND QUESTIONS

1. Exhibit 4-1 lists a number of possible reasons for the rapid growth
    of international charities in foreign aid. What other possible rea-
    sons can you add to this list? Write them down.
2. Using your own knowledge of international charities, rank-order
    the entire list in Exhibit 4-1 from the most important reasons for
    the rapid growth of NGOs in foreign aid to the least important rea-
    sons.
3. Compare and discuss your rankings with those of other learners.

References

Maren, M. (1997). *The road to hell: The ravaging effects of foreign aid and international charity*. New York: Free Press.
Rieff, D. (1997). Charity on the rampage. *Foreign Affairs, 76*(1): 132–138.

5

Nonprofit Board Governance

DELTA COMMUNITY LIBRARY

Delta Community Library is housed in one location. It has a full-time staff of 10 professional librarians and 5 staff positions, as well as some 40 volunteers performing a variety of duties. The library has a clear mission to meet the community's needs for sufficient books and periodicals. It has a solid and consistent budget that grows to meet inflation each year. Approximately 80 percent of its funding comes from direct amounts paid by the county and the three cities it serves. In addition, a variety of fundraising events throughout the year generates 10 percent of its budget, with the remaining funds coming from a small fee paid when joining the library and various library fines. Although it has instituted a couple of new projects in recent years (especially some children's activities), its role as a "traditional" library is clear and solid.

MOUNTAIN COMMUNITY ARTS CENTER

The Mountain Community Arts Center is only two years old. Its mission and goals have been very unstructured, and two executive directors have come and gone. The arts community is deeply divided on the center's purpose. Some see the center as a place for local artists to sell and practice their craft, while others envision the center as a leadership organization coordinating the direction of funding for arts in the community.

The Arts Center has a full-time director, two part-time art teachers, one part-time music teacher, and two support staff. In addition, the center has between five and forty volunteers, depending on the activity. Half of the Arts Center's budget (50 percent) is funded by a grant from the statewide arts council, 10 percent of its financial support comes from a discretionary account with the local city council, and the other 40 percent comes from a wide range of fees and "memberships."

INSTRUCTIONS AND QUESTIONS

1. What is the difference in board governance in these two organizations?
2. What do the boards need to do differently, and why?
3. What should be done by a new executive director in each organization, given the different levels of board maturity and understanding of their roles?
4. What do the two boards need to do first? Over the long term?

6

Metropolitan Emergency Medical Services

Every year, approximately 11,000 deaths occur in the Sunnyside metro area. Of these, 6,000 are attributed to sudden death: i.e., acute, sudden illness or injury. Authorities estimate that more than 500 lives could be saved each year through the use of a co-ordinated emergency medical services system that would ensure a uniform level of service for the entire region.

Metropolitan Emergency Medical Services (MEMS), a non-profit agency, became operational approximately ten years ago. To try to minimize the possibility of sudden death from illness or injury, a system was developed that would enable MEMS to dispatch the closest ambulance (public or private) to the scene of an emergency. MEMS provides a single seven-digit number for persons to report emergencies throughout the 17-county metropolitan area. The MEMS system, though technically well designed and staffed with qualified personnel, has no power to coerce participation and hence cannot authoritatively allocate the emergency calls that the ambulance firms depend on for their livelihood.

The MEMS system divides the 17-county metro area into eight disaster zones. The central disaster zone is at the core, and each of the other zones fans out from the central zone and is bisected by a major transportation artery. Within each disaster zone, a physician and one alternate have been assigned as the zone on-site medical director. In the event of a disaster, the zone director will assume control upon arrival at the scene. Each director is familiar with the specific medical resources and geography of his or her area and has complete knowledge of the MEMS communications system.

The MEMS communications system provides the zone director with a tremendous inventory of medical expertise. The MEMS center is a patchwork of communications equipment. The center provides for multiple communication modes: radio to telephone, radio to radio, telephone to radio, and telephone to telephone. These capabilities enable the MEMS coordinator to link a physician at the regional Poison Control Center, or to connect an emergency medical technician with a portable radio through to a physician at an emergency room or even at home. The MEMS system also enables area ambulances to talk directly with each other during a disaster. The MEMS system covers approximately 3,000 square miles, and its first major accomplishment was to reduce several hundred emergency telephone numbers to one.

The MEMS system received an initial grant of $400,000 from the Robert Wood Johnson Foundation. This grant, however, does not fully provide for the needs of the system, and through last year, MEMS received practically all its funding from a 15-cent-per-capita donation from five counties. It also received a federal Health and Human Services grant totalling $250,000 and other private grants in excess of $50,000.

A major budgetary setback occurred during the last fiscal year. Because some counties became unwilling to help meet its financial needs, MEMS was forced to reduce its budget by $133,000, nearly one-fourth of its operating budget.

The financial setback has multiple causes, which some details will help explain. MEMS uses a redundant computer system especially designed for its requirements. The computer automatically identifies the three nearest ambulances, shows their locations on a street map, and then coordinates and estimates the time of arrival for each ambulance. It also identifies the ambulance as either an advanced or a basic life-support unit. The MEMS communicator then selects the appropriate unit, or two if an advanced unit is required but is more than six minutes away. This information is transferred through video readouts to the ambulance dispatcher. The dispatcher then contacts the ambulance.

The location and status of vehicles, whether stationary or enroute, are monitored simultaneously, with the location of each vehicle updated automatically every 30 seconds from the last known position.

Participation in MEMS is voluntary on the part of the ambulance firms. These firms include both public and private ambulance services. Publicly supported ambulance services have been willing to participate freely in MEMS, but private operators have begun to express increasing reservations. Private operators at first were enthusiastic about MEMS, but they increasingly have come to believe that promises concerning the distribution of emergency calls have not been kept. Complex interests are at issue.

Fifteen ambulance services, public and private, participate in MEMS. There are 56 life-support units within the MEMS operation. Of these units, 20 belong to Gorham Memorial Hospital (public), and 18 belong to Sunnyside Ambulance Service (private). Two counties subsidize private firms in their areas, but the remaining counties do not. Some of the companies need additional business badly, while others do not; some receive funds to carry indigent patients, and others do not.

Some of the smaller companies say they are not getting enough calls to remain fiscally solvent. The small companies, each of which has two to four ambulances, contend that MEMS has reduced the number of calls they receive. This stems from the fact that the two largest ambulance providers—Gorham and Sunnyside—have allowed MEMS to place some of their vehicles at strategic locations. Often, this places a competing ambulance firm in the areas where the smaller firms once operated exclusively. MEMS has succeeded in providing a more efficient use of vehicles but as a byproduct has placed some of the smaller firms in a fiscally precarious situation. More than the immediate self-interest of the smaller firms may be involved. Their failure might decrease the number of ambulances and trained personnel available. The threatened companies contend that this would ultimately serve to lower the quality of emergency medical services throughout the entire system.

The dilemmas are clear to all observers. If MEMS provides adequate emergency medical coverage to the citizens in the 17 counties it serves, it may (and probably will) eventually force some of the providers of these services into positions that are not economically viable. But if MEMS does not shift some of the existing capacity, needless deaths will probably occur. The small ambulance firms, though their participation is voluntary, cannot afford to pull out. As the public becomes more aware of the MEMS emergency number, more and more citizens will rely solely on it. In fact, the fire and police departments of all 17 counties already use MEMS exclusively when requesting ambulance assistance. Thus, no small firm can afford to drop out of the program.

The larger providers have various stakes in MEMS. The Gorham ambulance service receives funds from county and federal governments, and therefore does not look to its ambulance service to generate income. Moreover, except for the drivers, Gorham ambulances are staffed with interns and student nurses, who receive little or no pay. Sunnyside Ambulance Service is in a different position. The only funds it receives are those earned from ambulance calls, and competition from Gorham via MEMS has its costs. But Sunnyside benefits from the fact that its once-underutilized capacity is now placed in a more productive location.

In sum, MEMS decisions are of extreme economic concern to the majority of the firms that participate in the program. In addition to the life-and-death calls that allow for the care and aid of citizens, MEMS faces decisions that could also mean life or death to some of the private firms involved in the program.

The crunch often comes in getting firms to respond to emergency calls. MEMS cannot force any ambulance firm to go anywhere it does not wish. This means, for example, that some areas, especially those of low income, do not have adequate coverage. Some counties compensate firms for the indigent calls they receive, but other counties do not.

This situation can sometimes have tragic results. Consider one emergency call, which occurs about 4:00 on a Wednesday afternoon. Mrs. Jones, who is visiting from another state, suffers an epileptic seizure. Her daughter requests an ambulance. The first MEMS call goes to a private ambulance three minutes away, which refuses the call because Mrs. Jones is in a poor section of an outlying county. The second closest ambulance, from the same firm, also refuses the call. The third and final ambulance listed on the computer readout belongs to a small, private firm. Its personnel, knowing they are not the closest ambulance to the scene of the emergency, ask why others did not take the call. When told about the refusal, they respond that they already have taken their fair share of similar cases.

The MEMS dispatcher runs through a second readout to find the next three nearest ambulances, all of which are more than 20 minutes away from the emergency. A Gorham ambulance is on the list, and since it is publicly financed, it will respond to this call. But many minutes have elapsed since the call about Mrs. Jones came through, and it will be another 22 to 25 minutes before the Gorham ambulance can reach her.

INSTRUCTIONS AND QUESTIONS

As the consultant who encouraged the Johnson Foundation's initial grant, you have a strong commitment to seeing MEMS work. You know that the system as designed depends on voluntary participation. But you also recognize that the system itself, however effective in operation, has forever altered the ethical responsibilities and legal obligations of the various possible participants.

1. Assume that MEMS is located in the state where you are reading this. Spend some time in a law library exploring the relevant portions of your state codes—health and welfare, criminal (penal), government, and civil (business licenses, torts), and so on—to identify the local obligations of public and private ambulance services and the powers of regional and local authorities in these matters. Prepare a brief summary of your findings.

2. Now develop a strategy to eliminate the problem of refused calls. Be as specific as you need to be, including drafting statutory amendments and a strategy for assuring their adoption.

7

A Do-Gooder Gets Done In: Mary T's View of a Support Group

Mary T had come to grips with two aspects of her new condition: the nest was now empty, and she had been diagnosed with a serious but not life-threatening disease.

She decided to get back into volunteering—specifically, by searching for a support group to help fellow sufferers of the disease she now shared. Mary T had received plenty of support and encouragement from her family, but she possessed a continuing desire to help others in their quest for support and encouragement. Now she wanted to help her fellow sufferers gain knowledge that would assist them in coping with the puzzling disease they shared.

Mary T's needs were also bounded by a desire to avoid first-banana roles. Her disease diminished her energy, for one thing. Moreover, she and her husband had elaborate post-retirement plans to travel, often overseas and for extended periods. Thus, Mary T wanted some involvement, but not too much.

Mary T soon discovered a vehicle suitable for her needs: a group of six or seven people who had been meeting for a few months in a church basement. The leader, Helen, had a severe case of the disease suffered by all members. She walked with some difficulty, was unable to hold a full-time job, and had adopted a new life-style because of her illness. Helen was highly disciplined, intelligent, and caring. Mary T saw her as an excellent leader for the struggling Support Group (henceforth referred to as SG).

The SG was no casual association for Helen. "This is the only thing I do in my life," she confessed to Mary T one day. "This *is* my life." The words rang true. Helen was a widow with no children, and she had time and energy available for the SG. For example, when someone in the SG was hospitalized or took sick, Helen would phone them, send greetings, and visit. Sometimes she would prepare a meal for the sick member, despite her own great difficulties. Helen also would send cards and notes throughout the year, as when thanking Mary T for her inspirational devotionals and her help in other SG work.

For her part, Mary T was delighted with the SG, and especially with Helen. Mary T was committed to the SG but, unlike Helen, it was not the center of her life. Far from it, in fact. Mary T had an extensive travel schedule, she doted on a growing batch of grandchildren, and her health at times encouraged her to pull back from her local activities. Thus, Helen was perfect for Mary T, willingly doing most of the consistently demanding work but leaving room for Mary T.

Given Helen's good example, Mary T's SG involvement soon grew. Mary T served on two SG committees, called members between meetings to see how they were doing, sent cards and notes to ailing members, and led meetings in Helen's absence. She also spent a good deal of time talking with SG members, usually before and after meetings, about little things as well as about their triumphs and tragedies. Mary T also was encouraged to become a member of the Regional Board of Directors. As such, she served as the liaison between the Board and the SG, which reinforced her ties to Helen. Mary T also wrote articles concerning the SG for the Board's monthly newsletter. Subsequently, Mary T also played an increasing role in fundraising for the SG, for its Regional Office as well as the National Foundation Office sponsoring the SG.

A SUPPORT GROUP TAKES OFF

After several months of holding meetings for an expanding list of attendees that had outgrown the church meeting room, the members of the SG were offered a new meeting site. Flip, a full-time supervisor at a local health care facility (HCF), suggested a move to his employer's quarters in the hope of further expanding the group and thus helping more people.

All SG members were in favor of this suggestion. Flip had recently become an active and helpful member of the rapidly growing SG. He came not as a fellow sufferer but as an HCF employee who had been given the task of improving his organization's outreach. Flip's status proved no drawback. He enthusiastically shared his expanding knowledge of the disease, helped acquire speakers from his HCF, and generally supported and encouraged all SG members.

After Flip had obtained permission for the SG to meet monthly at his HCF, his involvement increased even further. He first joined Helen—and progressively took over most of the responsibility—in arranging for good speakers, and he arranged for delicious, nutritious, and inexpensive SG lunches prepared by the HCF, complete with snacks and drinks before the meeting. Flip also became SG vice president and, along with Helen, took major responsibility for producing an enhanced newsletter for the SG.

Helen at first directed this new activity. As SG leader, she announced that officers would be elected and specified the committees to be formed. In addition, she recruited people for each position "to keep the SG active."

Not surprisingly, Helen was elected president. Flip became vice president, and Emily was chosen as treasurer. Emily was a new member and a very good friend of Helen's and later became a member of the Board who helped with fundraising. She had a severe case of the disease and, like Helen, made the SG a big part of her life. Mary T declined to run for SG office but remained on the Regional Board.

One of the new cast of characters came as a bit of a surprise: Marilyn, the new regional director. The Foundation appointed her to a paid position that had been vacant—forever, it seems.

After her appointment, Marilyn made a point of attending every meeting of both the SG and the Regional Board. She grew increasingly active and provided important input concerning the disease and the Foundation's various levels: regional, state, national, and international.

Busier than ever, Helen continued to prepare energetically for SG meetings. With Flip, she planned interesting, instructive, and inspirational programs. Mary T especially remembers one such meeting, when the speaker, a quadriplegic, brought tears to the eyes of many as he related the story of his life of amazing accomplishments despite severe physical handicaps.

The SG went very well at the HCF for about two years. Enrollment increased from a beginning of 5 or 6 to a turnout of 40 or 50 at some meetings. Members seemed delighted with the new SG: they gained knowledge, inspiration, support, encouragement, and love from each other, as well as many benefits from the programs. The luncheons were a special treat and a pleasant time of welcome fellowship.

Best of all for most SG members, everyone seemed to get along. Helen was a committed, forceful, and effective leader. Mary T was well liked and respected for her considerable work with the group including some creative initiatives. Flip was a tremendous vice president, helping in every possible way. Emily continued to be a close friend of Helen's and a big help to the SG, especially in fund-raising activities. Marilyn was well accepted as regional director, although she voiced ambitions for bigger roles for herself in the Foundation.

A STONE IN HELEN'S SHOE, OR A BOULDER?

The group's dynamics soon began to shift. Following one regular meeting of the SG, some of the leaders—Helen, Flip, Emily, Marilyn, and Mary T—were sitting around a table making plans. In the course of the conversation, Marilyn said, in effect: "When the leadership changes, we will do such-and-such." Flip and Emily outwardly appeared to agree with Marilyn's remark, and they were the most powerful members of the SG, after Helen.

Helen and Mary T were shocked. In her own eyes, Helen had been an exemplary leader, and she often mused out loud that only death could cut short her service to the SG in her present position. Helen was so stunned by the suggestion that she did not say anything for the next 15 minutes, which was very much out of character. Mary T, who had grown close to Helen, also did not respond at the time.

The small meeting soon dispersed without any response to Marilyn's remark. Helen and Mary T walked to the parking lot in complete silence, broken only at the last moment by Mary T asking Helen what she thought about Marilyn's remark. Helen admitted hurt, disappointment, and utter amazement—the SG was going very well, and she felt that she had been doing an excellent job. Mary T agreed with Helen wholeheartedly, and both continued their conversation in Helen's car. Perhaps *the* central remark was Helen's: "Things were better before we had a regional director. Marilyn's playing too big a role in our SG. What does she think she's doing?"

Their conversation concluded with Mary T asking to be kept informed. Soon thereafter, Helen phoned Marilyn, and she followed up with a call to Morris, chief executive at the Foundation's National Office to explain her displeasure with Marilyn's statement. Morris listened patiently but gave Helen no overt signals.

Helen and Mary T spoke on the phone many times in the succeeding weeks. Mary T usually just listened sympathetically as Helen expressed feelings of hurt, anger, and disbelief. Increasingly, however, Mary T felt ineffective in "talking through" Helen's concerns.

Things seemed to get worse for Helen. On a few occasions, she exploded. One time to nobody in particular, she complained: "Flip wants my job, so he kisses up to the health care facility employing him." On occasion, Marilyn was the target. "Where was the Regional Office when we were struggling? Now, she wants to take credit for what we have done."

Helen's language could become sulfurous during these explosions, which occurred several times in public settings. Even Mary T grew concerned. Most SG members were surprised and disturbed by the outbursts.

These outbursts grew to be a dark lining of an otherwise silver cloud. In the SG, there certainly was plenty going on for which credit might be appropriate, or even sought after. Under Helen's aggressive leadership, average attendance at monthly meetings had been doubling or tripling each year. Not only were the speakers very good or even excellent, but the SG now met in a comfortable setting, with a great meal for a small price. Moreover, income from a local 5-K walk/run sponsored by the SG had increased from $2,500 to more than $12,000.

MOVING TOWARD A CHANGE OF LEADERSHIP

These achievements initially were a source of pride for all, but opinions began to change. More and more talk, on the Board and elsewhere, came to focus on Helen and her "unilateral ways." Helen saw much or all of this as an effort to deprive her of "my life's work."

More or less unanimously, but reluctantly, SG members decided that Helen should be given the opportunity to meet with the local Board of Directors, of which Flip, Emily, and Mary T were now members. Marilyn, as regional director, was always invited but did not have a vote. Probably on Marilyn's initiative, Morris also was invited. He was chief executive of the Foundation supporting the SG.

The initial sense of purpose differed. Mary T saw the session as an opportunity for Helen to air her grievance with the Board of Directors. Others saw the meeting as Helen's last chance to defend her actions and perhaps to promise to do better.

Perhaps by accident, the seating at the meeting suggested an adversarial quality. Mary T arrived early and took a chair from among those placed in a large circle. Mary T recalls being surprised that there seemed to be "too many chairs for the likely attendees." Soon, she was surrounded. Flip and Emily sat next to Mary T on one side. Marilyn and Morris, arriving together, soon flanked Mary T on the other side. Other board members also clustered together. Only a few minutes before the meeting began, Helen and two of her loyal supporters in the SG walked in and sat directly opposite a closed semicircle.

The Board chair opened the meeting and explained his view of its purpose: to air Helen's concerns about Marilyn's statement concerning possible changes in SG leadership. Then he asked Helen to state her concerns. Helen immediately began shouting: "Flip wants my job. He wants to be the SG leader. He's been trying to run things for awhile now. He's been trying to take over. He wants my job."

Mary T was stunned by Helen's outburst. She could understand Helen's deep disappointment over the regional director's suggestion of a new leadership, but Mary T deeply disapproved of Helen's lashing out at Flip. Despite her friendship with Helen, Mary T felt Flip had been doing a great job. Moreover, Mary T had been unaware of Helen's feelings about Flip. It was only later that Mary T learned that Helen earlier had named Flip as her competitor. To be sure, Flip was a full-time worker at the HCF where the SG meetings were now held, and an active SG officer as well as Board member. But Mary T truly believed that SG primary leadership was far from Flip's mind. Indeed, on hearing Helen's reaction for the first time, she remembers thinking: "That doesn't sound right. If anybody, I'd guess it would be Marilyn. Those two had real differences, but Flip was just an eager problem-solver."

After a bit, in any case, Flip caught his breath. He was, he admitted, extremely surprised, disappointed, and even deeply hurt by Helen's outburst. In a polite and composed manner, Flip emphasized that he never had any intention of taking Helen's position. In fact, even if the leadership were offered to him, he would not accept. He had just learned yesterday from his wife that "they were pregnant," and Flip was not looking for new responsibilities. Indeed, the pair had planned an active parenting role for Flip, and he probably would be seeking time off from HCF under the applicable federal legislation.

Helen was not mollified by Flip's response. She just kept lashing out against him. Morris urged a "cooling-off period."

As people were leaving, Helen took Mary T by the sleeve. "Call me," she half-requested and half-commanded. "I will," Mary T replied, but she couldn't do it. Mary T always tried to keep her word but, after troubled reflections on Helen's recent behavior, could not make that call to Helen.

Several weeks later, Morris called a special meeting to give Helen the opportunity to explain matters to a broader audience: the entire SG. Flip, Emily, Marilyn, Morris, and Mary T all attended, along with a surprising number of members of the SG. Helen talked about the leadership situation in an excited tone, albeit muted in comparison to the meeting with the Board of Directors. This meeting was held in a local restaurant. Helen strongly attacked Flip, along with Marilyn, for suggesting a possible change in leadership. She also made a negative comment concerning Mary T, to which Mary T did not respond, but which she felt.

Morris tried to smooth over the situation. There was a brief discussion concerning the possibility of forming two local SGs, but nothing definite was decided.

MAJOR CHANGES IN LEADERSHIP

This meeting, and several more, had direct effects. The local Board did not act, but Morris and the Foundation got a clear message to Helen: neither the Foundation nor HCF would support this SG with Helen at the helm. The reason: her unacceptable behavior at the meeting with the Board. So, in effect, Helen was banned from the SG at the HCF.

Helen proceeded to form SG-II at a different facility, not far away but in a different Foundation region. She took with her three members from the original SG. Virtually all SG members chose to stay at the HCF because of the high quality of the meetings.

Emily—not Flip, as Helen had suspected—became the new SG leader. In any case, after a few months, Emily moved out of state. Marilyn got a substantial promotion to Foundation headquarters and was soon gone.

Flip continued to help SG-I in every way possible. Mary T believed that Helen's charges had a profound effect upon him. In any case, Flip and his wife had a beautiful baby, and, after a period of leave for early parenting, he got a major promotion in the HCF, where he now heads all of their substantial outreach programs. Flip is no longer very active in SG-I, but the meetings continue to be held at the HCF.

EXIT, ONE WOUNDED DO-GOODER

The dynamics leading to these changes had proved to be far more than Mary T wanted or could handle. Before the Foundation had taken action, the local Board had considered whether Helen should continue as the head, and most members had been moving toward a decision that Helen step down. Mary T would have voted "abstain" on Helen's continuation, if it went that far, although she agreed that things had gone too far for Helen to continue.

Before any Board decision, but after several meetings, Helen had resigned from SG-I and started SG-II.

Mary T also soon left, reacting to health problems she attributes to "the troubles." About the time of the first Board meeting, she started to ache all over, feeling much distress. Trying to cope sapped Mary T's energy. The pain also caused much sleeplessness, which in turn produced fatigue. A measure of her disease's activity soared.

Her doctor changed Mary T's medications, but nine months passed before Mary T returned to where she had been before the "flare-up." During this period, Mary T was distressed about what had happened to Helen. She wondered if she could have done more to help during Helen's time of trial. In fact, Mary T still wonders about this. She has reduced her volunteer efforts and avoids working in groups. She does not wish to be "burned" again.

INSTRUCTIONS AND QUESTIONS

1. Do you see many volunteers like Mary T or Helen? If so, what can supervisory units do to prepare them for conflict and its constructive resolution? Or would that be meddling?

2. What might Mary T have done differently, and when? How do you react to her coping? What advice would you give her?

3. Make some reasonable guesses about events after Morris became involved in the questioning of Helen's role.

4. Review one of the numerous texts on conflict resolution. Do they have any relevance for cases like this one?

References

Dana, D. (1989). *Managing differences*. Wolcott, CT: MTI Publications.

Dana, D. (1990). *Talk it out*. Amherst, MA: Human Resource Development Press.

Walton, R. (1987). *Interpersonal peacemaking*. Reading, MA: Addison-Wesley.

8

Images of Third-Sector Organizations and Participants

People form perceptions of individuals and of organizations that can influence attitudes and behaviors. For example, if people believe you are friendly, they will be predisposed to think positively of you and approve of what you do. Even substantial evidence to the contrary may not change these assumptions. Most of us also hold some unexamined attitudes about members of different kinds of organizations.

INSTRUCTIONS AND QUESTIONS

This application encourages you to generalize about three kinds of organizations and their members. There are no correct answers, but the following exercises may be useful:

1. Rank-order (1 to 3) the following list of descriptors as they apply to each of the three major organizational sectors: voluntary, business, and public.
2. Look for patterns of differences/similarities in the three sets of descriptors.
3. What are the implications of any patterns for how you feel about and act toward organizations or people in the three arenas?

4. Can you think of ways to test your stereotypes? For example, discuss your list with one or two other people who also have completed Exercises 1–3.

Exhibit 8-1.

Possible Descriptors	Voluntary Organizations	Business Organizations	Public Organizations
a. Friendly			
b. Cut-throat competition			
c. Highly qualified members			
d. Wasteful and uneconomical			
e. Creative and innovative			
f. Low energy level			
g. Recruits rejects or marginal performers			
h. Members have good hearts			
i. Strong ethical and moral sense			
j. Fuzzy minds dominate			
k. Dollars dominate decision-making			
l. Hard-headed and practical			
m. Do good things			

9

Why a "Third Sector"?

In these days of "What's in it for me?" the existence of a robust and growing nonprofit and voluntary sector deserves close attention. Exhibit 9-1 lists several reasons for the origin and continued existence of this third-sector arena, which variously augments and provides an alternative to the two other conventional sectors, business and government.

Exhibit 9-1.   Reasons for a Robust Third Sector

---

1. Historical Explanation
As Brudney (1996) notes, "In an age in which citizens have routinely come to expect government to act in their interest in social and economic life, it may be difficult to recall that in most countries, society preceded the establishment of the state." The voluntary sector has traditionally provided many goods and services: cultural, health-related, housing, charity, and welfare, among many others.

Many factors preserved this early motivation. Many citizens remained skeptical or perhaps suspicious about government, even as they accepted or eagerly sought its intervention. Today's politics reflect just such skepticism or suspicion, and this helps fuel the current growth in third-sector activities.

2. Market Failure
Markets can fail in several senses. Thus, recession or depression can ravage a citizenry. In addition, markets work differently in different

10

Rethinking Our Approach to Poverty[1]

America no longer can escape the truth: three decades of social welfare policies have failed, condemning too many of our citizens to lives of despair. We are a compassionate society that will help the truly needy. In the mid-1960s, the prevailing view was that this goal could be accomplished through high-rise bureaucracies in Washington. Unfortunately, the Great Society set us on a path that has been an unmitigated disaster, a disaster more harmful to more Americans than the Vietnam War.

Newt Gingrich[2]

Over the past 30 years, we have waged a five-trillion-dollar War on Poverty. And yet, when we look at the murder rate in our inner cities; the cocaine, heroin, and crack addiction destroying countless young lives; the illiteracy rate; and the number of children who have never known a father, we can see clearly that the

---

[1]Originally published in *Phi Kappa Phi Journal*, Summer 1996, 76(3): 9–12, 19. Reprinted with permission of author.

[2]Newt Gingrich (R-Ga.) is Speaker of the House of Representatives. He represents the Sixth Congressional District in the State of Georgia.

current approach to helping the poor has exacted a cost far greater than mere money. The system is in urgent need of renewal. Renewal means replacing what has become a culture of poverty and violence with one of productivity and safety—not just helping the poor or focusing on the inner cities, but actually replacing one culture with another. More than just a War on Poverty, we must be prepared to wage a multi-faceted War on Urban Despair.

Efforts to repair or improve the current welfare system are doomed to fail if they sidestep the holistic nature of the problem. In a holistic model, everything has to be taken into account, unlike in a reductionist model, which breaks a problem down into a series of building blocks and decides which piece to deal with first. There is a very big difference between the two. In the holistic model, every piece depends on every other piece. You must deal with the totality, or it does not work.

Piecemeal efforts to repair our system and its culture of poverty and violence are doomed to fail. We ask the poor, "Why don't you go to work?" And they say, "Fine." But if they do go to work, they lose Medicaid. Thus, if one of their children gets sick, they promptly lose all the money they just earned. If they receive food stamps or AFDC, the government punishes them if they try to save any money. They can do nothing that actually improves their lives. We have an interlocking system in which change to any one piece without thinking through change to the whole is pointless.

In the 1960s, we tried a deal that did not work. Well-meaning, sincere people said, "Send a check to the IRS, and your government will hire somebody smart enough to save people for you." It failed. The government ended up hiring people who cannot save anybody. These people would like to help, but the rules and regulations do not let them. Then more people are hired to not do their job, and the average citizen sends a bigger check to the IRS. Meanwhile, more people decay because if you are not improving your life every day, you are decaying. A person does not remain stable—you either grow or you shrink. We have had, now, thirty years of shrinking human beings in the name of bureaucracy.

We must find a way to address the problems of the whole person. A substantive difference exists between the future we want to create and the future that the Washington bureaucracy has tried and failed to create. We believe the focus must be on changing and saving people; we are not interested in maintaining them in their decay. The goal should not be how to maintain the poor, the addicted, or the alcoholic. The goal must be how to save them.

PAVING NEW PATHS

We cannot save "the poor"—an amorphous, faceless group—but we can save a Sally; we can save a Fred; we can save a Betty. The business of transforming human beings in the end is one person dealing with one person at a time. It cannot be anonymous bureaucrats filling out forms on people they do not know, do not care about, and will not remember. The new model requires more missionaries and fewer bureaucrats.

Our current education crisis is a good example. As a college professor, I love teaching. But I believe that it is a missionary activity. You take people without civilization, and you hope to convert them to civilization. The more we have bureaucratized teaching, the more we have destroyed it. All social work in the end is missionary work. If that is not understood, you cannot understand what is going on with human beings.

This means, first, that our approaches have to be locally based. Recently, more than eighty groups from across the country came to Washington in support of the Community Renewal project. Republicans understand that our new approach cannot be Washington-directed. Though it is no fault of their own, the secretaries or undersecretaries of this Washington department or that Washington agency have no idea who is or is not being saved. The only thing they have—the only thing we all have—are the statistics of failure.

Second, I sincerely believe that if we do not at least encourage a faith-based approach, our efforts ultimately will be fruitless. Just as with the Alcoholics Anonymous first step—you have to come to the realization that there is a Creator, a being greater than yourself—people cannot solve their problems "inside themselves." Or, consider the example of Habitat for Humanity, which has a motto of "Growing a family, while building a house." People getting Habitat houses are required to work for 100 hours on other people's homes, for 300 hours on their own, and take a 20-hour course on "home maintenance." They pray before they get the house and receive a Bible as part of the ceremony. Habitat, as a result, has become one of the more successful approaches to combating the problems of low-income housing. It is not about just giving people a house to move into; it is about instilling them with life-affirming habits that encourage them to achieve beyond themselves.

We are not talking about a small change. If we truly want healthy inner cities, if we truly want healthy Indian reservations, and if we truly want healthy West Virginia Appalachian poor neighborhoods, we are talking about one of the largest changes ever to be contemplated in American history. And we have to take it seriously. We must decide in our generation that we are fed up with a system that encourages us to regret death or impoverishment but will not change to prevent it. We must do something to replace this failed system. Our goal should be to wake up one morning with the certainty that not one single child died during the night in a public housing project.

COMMUNITY RENEWAL: THE GOVERNMENT ROLE

Clearly, government does have a role in fighting poverty—but its primary role is to remove the barriers that exist now to the natural forms of poverty intervention that worked for centuries. Secondly, where possible, government can create an incentive system to allow the poor to help themselves without heaping further burdens upon them. Finally, government must recognize that it is incapable of truly transforming lives and that it should get out of the way and allow those who are capable to do the job. Toward those ends the Republican reform effort is already underway.

Our first major measure, the Housing Act of 1996, passed the House of Representatives in May. This bill boosts home ownership and creates an environment in which families can be employed without losing other benefits and can make their own housing choices. It also creates incentives for entrepreneurship on the part of housing authorities and residents.

The most significant legislation that the 104th Congress will attempt to pass this year is the Community Renewal Project: a three-part approach to identifying and finding real solutions to the problems of poverty-afflicted areas.

Personal Economic Empowerment Act

The Personal Economic Empowerment Act begins by creating 100 "Renewal Communities." To qualify, communities must have a poverty rate of 20 percent or more and an unemployment rate at least one-and-a-half times the national rate, and at least 70 percent of the households in the community must have incomes below 80 percent of the median income of households. The community also must have experienced a population decline of 20 percent or more between 1980 and 1990. The Act further requires local communities to reduce tax rates and fees within zones and eliminate state and local sales taxes to be eligible for community designation. Other provisions include the following:

- Requirements for state and local governments to waive local occupational licensing regulations and other barriers to entry, except those explicitly needed to protect health and safety.
- Creation of federal tax incentives for renewal communities, including an elimination of capital gains taxes on investments in stock, business property, or partnerships within zones as long as the assets are held for five years or longer. The bill includes tax credits for commercial revitalization and allows for individuals to take a deduction for the purchase of business stock within the zones. Finally, the bill will include a business tax credit for hiring disadvantaged workers.
- Ability for states and local governments to request waivers from oppressive federal regulations within the zones.
- Permission for banks to meet their Community Reinvestment Act requirements by lending money to qualified community development intermediaries. It will allow banks to meet their

obligations by working with lending institutions and neighborhood groups.

Family Renewal Act

The Family Renewal Act will include school-choice provisions. It creates public charter schools and provides low-income "scholarships" that will go only to students whose families are at or below 185 percent of the poverty rate. The scholarships can cover the costs of tuition or transportation to any private, public, or parochial school in a renewal community zone. Other provisions of the bill are:

- A charitable contribution tax credit worth $100 for donations to a qualified charity.
- The creation of Family Development Accounts to allow low-income people to build an account similar to an IRA, with deposits matched by the federal government. Withdrawals could be used only for one of three purchases: a home, postsecondary education, or the creation of a small business.

Neighborhood Group Empowerment Act

The Neighborhood Group Empowerment Act requires all federal drug treatment programs to provide vouchers so that people seeking help can use neighborhood groups if they choose. The measure:

- Ends restrictions against faith-based counseling or neighborhood groups;
- Removes "credentialing" and other barriers so that neighborhood groups can qualify as legitimate drug abuse treatment providers;
- Requires all grantees to demonstrate accountability by developing objective measures of how well these groups promote real change in people's lives;
- Authorizes a General Accounting Office report to compare the success rates of faith-based neighborhood groups as opposed to the traditional government-funded approach.

THE NEW MISSIONARIES

The kind of cultural change we are talking about requires not bureaucrats, but missionaries. It requires the kind of person who will sit steadfastly at 3:00 in the morning holding the hand of someone who is about to commit suicide. A bureaucracy cannot do that. Yes, there are some wonderful government employees; you do find people who are individually fabulous. But you cannot recruit people to a bureaucracy on the premise that they will stay there as long as needed. On the other hand, you can recruit to a volunteer organization on that premise. The two are very different models. Yet we sometimes get mad at bureaucracy, asking it to do things it cannot do, instead of distinguishing between those things government can do well and those things some other part of society can do better.

The War on Urban Despair must be waged by New Missionaries, individuals freed from the regulations that restrict bureaucrats from saving lives. They will be able to use all the resources available to them including, in particular, faith to restore humanity to lost souls. Several individuals have already signed up for the mission:

- Bob Cote is the founder and executive director of Step 13, a Denver transitional living program for alcohol and drug addicted individuals. Step 13 does not accept federal, state, or city funding. Instead, Step 13 developed a program in which all clients work and pay $120 per month and have established an in-house recycling business.
- Freddie Garcia, a former drug addict, now an ordained minister, established the Victory Fellowship of Texas, a Christian rehabilitation center. In the past 30 years more than 13,000 men and women have been treated and freed from drug and alcohol addiction by Victory Fellowship, which has expanded to 65 satellite centers in New Mexico, Texas, Puerto Rico, and Peru.
- Hanna Hawkins began nine years ago providing hot meals, clothing, and a number of other services to members of her southeast Washington, D.C., community. As word spread, more people came for assistance, and her services outgrew her home. She now cares for 140 children in two abandoned

apartments, where she gives well-balanced meals, clothing, personal-hygiene lessons, and Bible studies to those in need.

These individuals are living proof that our solutions to helping the poor lie not with the failed welfare state, but with a true opportunity society. We want to return power to the taxpayer, to the citizen, and to the community and allow true reform to germinate at the grassroots level. The community Renewal Project—the principles of which we are committed to seeing enacted well beyond this Congress—and the New Missionaries are vivid examples of how different our approach is from those of our friends who failed. They failed, not because they are bad people, but because they had ideas that simply did not work.

Those of us putting forward a new model understand the enormity of the task ahead. We know that change does not happen overnight; what we face is nothing less than the transformation of human lives—a slow, methodical process. But we must begin now. We have already lost too many lives by following the ill-fated policies of the past three decades. The time for committed renewal is today.

INSTRUCTIONS AND QUESTIONS

1. How do you respond to Newt Gingrich's basic position?
2. Whether you like that position or not, assume that Gingrich's view prevails in American politics. Take any nonprofit or voluntary organization of your choice, and try to fit it to Gingrich's template.
3. How would your target organization differ after attempts to fit its policies and practices to Gingrich's view?
4. In what ways would your target organization remain pretty much unchanged?

SECTION 2

Key Dimensions of Organizing and Managing Nonprofit, Voluntary, and Third-Sector Organizations

11

Dinosaurs Are Extinct: Should the Museum Be, Too?

PART ONE

In 1993, The Ivy Museum of Natural History and Science opened its doors amid much fanfare. With artifacts in place and the windows adorned with lights, the Ivy Museum opened its brand-new $43-million facility in splendor. Marketed to the public as the largest history and science museum of its kind, the site offered new technical innovations and advancements, including interactive exhibits and on-line access.

During the museum's early days, enthusiasm and anticipation ran high among city residents, visitors, academics, politicians, and children of all ages. The city newspaper, *The Peach Constitution and Journal*, described the museum as having "opened with a bang—one where the parking lots could not handle the throngs!" Mary Durn, the executive director, said with the similar passion that marked her quest to build a premier museum in Peachville: "I LOVE IT!" Furthermore, museum curators and the board of trustees were truly excited and hopeful about the museum, its offerings, and future prospects.

Although the museum's sparkling new multi-million-dollar brick facility gave an impression of solidity, its financial status was built on shaky ground. Little did the public know that the museum faced a debt of $21 million. One year after its opening, attendance and public enthusiasm began to drop precipitously. It was calculated that the museum would lose $1.5 million per year, strangled by the debt that museum trustees had secured to build the museum. By May 1994, the monetary crisis had become apparent when the museum missed a $1.3-million loan payment to Gynclays Bank PLC, the major creditor.

Soon Gynclays Bank began to move toward foreclosure. Within days, rumors and whispers concerning Gynclays' plan surfaced among the city's business community. Peach City History Center Director, Robert Hair, a colleague of Mary Durn, went on record with the statement: "I cannot imagine an institution starting with that kind of debt and not having a difficult time financially." In 1994, anonymous allegations against Ivy officials surfaced, but a subsequent audit cleared them of any wrongdoing.

Nevertheless, the allegations scarred Durn's reputation. The trustees left her in charge of getting exhibits, working on collections, and developing educational programs, while they hired F. Lee Burns to oversee the museum's overall operations and finances. Burns and the trustees requested that Gynclays provide additional time to pay off the interest as well as principal on $20 million in bonds that were issued five years prior. They also asked Democratic officeholders—the governor and state lawmakers—for financial help.

The governor hoped to help the museum by purchasing it with state lottery money, although state law required that lottery money be earmarked for education. Nonetheless, the governor urged Democratic leaders to purchase the museum and allow the Ivy Museum, Inc., a nonprofit organization that runs the museum, to continue operating it in a kind of public-private partnership.

INSTRUCTIONS AND QUESTIONS

1. Who is responsible for this crisis: the board of trustees, Durn, or the public?

2. What kind of oversight and fiduciary responsibilities should the museum's Board of Trustees have?

PART TWO

The governor requested a $6 million allocation for the museum. Although the allocation was aggressively pushed by the lieutenant governor, the request soon became a sticking point within the budget. Legislators did not believe that they could sell the idea to voters at a time when the state was privatizing some assets and downsizing others. House Appropriations Committee Chair Jerry Coles protested, "We just don't think we can afford it!" The Democrat Speaker of the House refused to agree to the allocation. After a long debate, the lieutenant governor was forced to yield in order to break the deadlock. Harold Books, Democratic state senator and chairman of the Senate Appropriations Committee, stated, "We still like the idea of the Ivy Museum, but quite frankly, in a tight budget year we need to look at it in more detail. It's dead as far as this budget is concerned."

Failure to fund the museum must have had more to do with priorities than money, however, because ultimately legislators found more than $12 million to fund last-minute additions, especially for items that pertained to the impending World Fair that was coming to the city. The governor was forced to abandon his larger plan for the Ivy Museum during the session.

Museum officials were stunned by the news. The chairman of the Ivy Museum's board of trustees, Ben Genderschaft IV, explained, "We had put a lot of time into it; we thought the support was there." He was quoted by the local paper as having said, "If they can get out from the burden of debt, they should have a real chance to be a viable institution."

Gynclays' plan for foreclosure would soon become reality. Museum trustees and officials continued to lobby the governor for relief. The attendance during 1994 was estimated at approximately 450,000 visitors. This figure was approximately 50,000 short of the total the museum had hoped to attract with its dinosaur exhibit. Continuing to urge the banks and Gynclays to extend the museum a grace period, Genderschaft hoped to offer another exhibit that would bring in additional funds. Genderschaft stated in a press conference, "We're by no means in a position where the museum is in jeopardy. It may just take us a little longer to get where we need to be!"

INSTRUCTIONS AND QUESTIONS

You are a member of the Ivy Museum's board of trustees.

1. What suggestions will you make concerning sources of funding?
2. Do you think your executive director, Genderschaft, is overly optimistic about the museum's prospects for survival?
3. Was the government wrong? Should the State have given the required funding to the museum?

CONCLUSION

Headlines in the local paper reported that the Ivy Museum of Natural History and Science, which had faced more than $20 million in debt, was now *debt free*. The debt was wiped out as a result of a $10-million gift from the Teddy W. Roosevelt Foundation, plus the willingness of seven banks to write off the rest of the debt.

"It's just a huge day for us to have that lifted off our shoulders," stated Ben Genderschaft IV. Although the Ivy Museum would not identify the Roosevelt Foundation as the source of the gift, a representative of the Foundation stated: "We are going to save the day! We think it's a thing worth keeping in private hands, and we have so much money in it already." The Roosevelt Foundation, which had already given $15 million to help build the $45-million museum, was characterized as a second solution.

According to Genderschaft, "We had explored every other avenue with the banks and the state." Before agreeing to the donation, the Foundation had requested that the Board of Trustees obtain commitments from other corporations and foundations to help pay the museum's operating expenses by sponsoring exhibits. In response to the request, Soda-Soda, Universal Services, and Phonelocal signed on to help. Additionally, the Board secured a $1 million donation from the J. Burrow Foundation. The money was to be used toward a new endowment. *The Peach Constitution and Journal* summed up the situation as follows:

> The Ivy Museum's legacy, Genderschaft said, is that the corporate and philanthropic communities now understand that no museum can be expected to open with debt. Museums need all their revenues to pay day-to-day expenses. Last year, the Ivy Museum was able to meet its annual $8 million in operating expenses and pay the banks $800,000 toward the debt.

INSTRUCTIONS AND QUESTIONS

1. What does this case imply about nonprofit planning? Responsibilities of the board of trustees? The role of the community and corporations?

2. What do you think of private-public partnerships? Should a museum be a public or private good?

References

Kettl, D.F. (1993). *Sharing power: Public governance and private markets.* Washington, DC: Brookings Institution.

Olenick, A.J., and Olenick, P.R. (1991). *A nonprofit organization operating manual* (chapters 3–6). New York: The Foundation Center.

Rehfuss, J. (1989). *Contracting out in government: A guide to working with outside contractors.* San Francisco: Jossey-Bass.

Wolf, T. (1990). *Managing a nonprofit organization.* New York: Simon & Schuster.

12

Retraining Displaced and Older Workers*

You heard a little bit about the Massachusetts Software Council, so I won't spend much time giving you any background on that. We are a traditional trade association providing traditional and non-traditional services to our members. We do lots of programs throughout the year on international issues, sales and marketing issues, legal and financial issues to help the CEOs of software companies better manage and grow their companies.

We do a lot of research on the software industry. We are advocates in terms of public policy issues at both the state and federal levels, on behalf of the software industry, and we have several unique features.

We are the only trade association that I know about that has its own rock band made up of our board members. They're called "Look and Feel," which is a term used in the software industry. If your software looks and feels like anyone else's, you're in big trouble.

*©1995, American Association of Retired Persons. Transcript of a speech given by Joyce Plotkin, executive director of the Massachusetts Software Council. Reprinted with permission.

We also have an educational technology program which is pretty unique. We've created a book called *The Switched-On Classroom*, which is a technology planning guide for public schools.

After the completion of that book, which was very well-received and profiled in *The New York Times*, we created a second program called the Massachusetts Tech Corps, which recruits professionals from the technology industry to volunteer to work on technology-related projects in schools.

On October 10th, just a few weeks ago, President Clinton announced a national tech corps, the U.S. Tech Corps, based on our Massachusetts model. So we're really delighted about the success of that program.

THE SOFTWARE COUNCIL FELLOWSHIP PROGRAM

The program that you're most interested in hearing about is the Software Council Fellowship Program. This is a program that takes people that have been laid off from the hardware, defense, and electronics industries, and retrains them for jobs in the software industry.

These are people that have major barriers to re-employment. They're basically middle management professionals. Age, length of time unemployed, and obsolete skills are certainly issues for these people.

The goal in creating this program was not to fill a short-term need. It was really a long-term objective. We believe in the pendulum theory. We don't have an immediate shortage of people, but we think the pendulum will swing. And we may at some point have a major shortage of people for the software industry.

So we embarked on this program for the long-term impact of it.

The development phase of the project took about 18 months. We worked with several state agencies and members of the software industry to see what kind of a program would make sense.

We did a series of focus groups with human resource professionals from the software industry and with long-term unemployed technology professionals. What we learned is that the software industry hires people who have software company experience.

Now, this is partially a result of the fact that most of the software companies in the United States and Massachusetts are small companies. Something like 58 percent of the companies have ten or fewer people. So there was no training function to recruit people in and put them through some extensive kind of training course.

So software industry experience was very important.

The other thing we learned from the HR people was that the biggest barrier for these people was not really necessarily a skill set but a mind set. So we sought to create a program that would help overcome those two obstacles to get some software company experience on someone's résumé, and to help them understand the environment—how to work in a small, fast-growing, very entrepreneurial company.

The program is funded by three state agencies: the Industrial Services Program, which channels federal, dislocated worker money into Massachusetts; the Bay State Skills Corporation, which is a quasi-public training organization; and the Department of Employment and Training in Massachusetts.

Those are the three public sector partners, and they provided money, administrative help, and some staffing.

The private industry, the software industry, also supplied money for this program. The companies that participate in the program pay into a pool based on size of company. We have many companies that don't have their first product out the door, and don't have any revenues yet. So they pay a smaller monthly fee, approximately $1,000. And the larger companies pay about $2,500.

The requirements for getting into the program are that a Fellow has to have a minimum of ten years' experience in one of these dislocated industries. They have to be computer literate. I'm not talking about advanced programming languages here. I'm talking about spreadsheets and database, some familiarity with those kinds of programs.

Also, people have to have some functional expertise in an area, like marketing or quality assurance (QA), that they can bring to the table.

The average age of the Fellows in the program is 46. Even though 10 years is a minimum requirement in terms of years of experience, the reality is that most of these people have 20 years' experience in the industry. We have a lot of people in the program between the ages of 40 and 60, with most of them concentrated in the 40 to 44 age category, and 50 to 59. We have several people over 60 in the program, and some over 70 as well.

The program consists of essentially a six-month training course. The first several weeks is really an orientation to the software industry, where we bring in people who are involved in managing all aspects of a software company.

We deal with both the business aspects of the company and the technology aspects of the software industry. And we do a lot of team-building exercises to try to break down the behavior patterns that some of the people have that are coming from the very large companies.

As an example, one person came out of a downsized company to work in my office at the Software Council. She was there about two weeks, when she came in to me and said, "What are the formal methods of communication here?"

I said, "We only have four people. We don't have any formal methods of communication.

"We make decisions in the ladies' room, the kitchen, or anywhere else we need to." That's an example of the kind of mind set problem that we're talking about.

Following this three-month training, this core learning as we call it, this orientation to the software industry, the Fellows go to work on a project at a software company to give them the software company experience for their résumé.

I'll give you an example of the kind of project. We had a 15-person software company that was looking to develop an international marketing plan. They did not have the in-house expertise.

They ended up being matched with a person that had 20 years' experience in marketing and international marketing from Digital Equipment Corporation. That person knew how to write a marketing plan, how to go about doing the market research. What the person didn't know was the software industry market.

So the person brought functional expertise to the small company. The person spent five months researching the marketplace, and was able to put together a terrific marketing plan for this company. The person wasn't hired at the end of that, but did get a job in another software company.

So that's an example of the kind of project that goes on in this program.

They are actually on-site in the software company four days a week. The fifth day they come back to the program for what we call weekly learning days. This is sort of adult-focused, adult-centered learning.

The people in the program identify the areas that they want to know more about. Some of them want to know Windows 95. So we bring in people to show them about Windows 95.

One company had a legal problem they were going through, a copyright issue. So somebody wanted a better understanding of the intellectual property protection issues. So we supplied the lecturers.

We offer somewhere between four and six programs a year. There are about 20 to 24 people in a program.

Now, how do you get into the program? We do advertise and recruit people through the newspapers and word of mouth. We also get help from state government agencies and from the private sector.

But at the same time as we're advertising, we talk to the 1,948 software companies that are in Massachusetts right now. And we ask them for a description of a project that they might like to have done by a seasoned professional.

These companies submit a project description. We, on the other hand, are soliciting résumés from our potential Fellows. We do a paper screen of the résumés, and for each project that's submitted by a company, we send over between four and six résumés for each of the projects.

The company that has the project interviews any or all of the potential Fellows. And they decide which person they want to work on the project in their company. So people are selected into the program by virtue of the companies selecting them, not us or not any other kind of bureaucracy.

There are about 70 companies in Massachusetts that have hosted Fellows since the program began in March of '93, in such areas as international marketing, quality assurance, technical support, documentation, technical writing, and some in the area of administration and finance.

Does the program work? We think it has a pretty good track record. We have 125 graduates of the program. Eighty-five percent of them got jobs at the end of this program. Somewhere between a quarter and a half of them end up getting employed by the companies for which they do their projects.

And the rest, we work with them during their weekly learning days to help them on a personal marketing plan, interviewing techniques, and résumé writing to help them market themselves to the software industry.

For any of the Fellows that don't have a job by the end of the program, we circulate the résumés to the 1,900-plus software companies that we have in the state to try to help them get a job.

About 75 percent of the companies that hire these Fellows say that they would not have hired these people if they hadn't come through our program. Now, that goes back to what I said earlier about having software company experience on the résumé. Most of them do not have that experience, so our program helps overcome that.

It's not an age thing, per se. At least, that's been our experience. With the downsizing in the federal government and cutting back on all sorts of training moneys and things, we are relooking at the program and turning to a more market focus. We will begin to take people that are not coming through the dislocated worker programs.

We are going to market the program at a cost of about $3,500, and people can self-pay and get into the program that way as well.

There are other people that don't come from the downsizing industries, from education and finance, that are now interested in taking this program to get into our very fast-growing industry.

Just in Massachusetts alone, we have more than doubled the number of companies and employees in software in six years. We have gone from 800 companies to 1,948 in six years. We've gone from 46,000 people employed to 98,000 people employed in six years. So there are many folks interested in getting into this fast-growing industry.

This program has sort of taken on a life of its own. So we've essentially spun it off. The Software Council itself has a staff of five people, and we have spun off the fellowship program, and it's run by a staff of four people. They have their own office out on Route 128, and we use a lot of people from the industry to help out as guest lecturers on both the learning days and the initial three-week program.

We have found this program to be a win-win at a lot of levels. It's a win for the Fellows, because it really helps them transition into a new industry. It gives people a new lease on life. It's a win for the industry because we get seasoned professionals. And it's a win for the government in that these people are gainfully employed.

We have a Fellow that had been unemployed for some time. He has a degree from MIT. He is physically challenged in that he is in a wheelchair, and he had some rough times. He essentially had a pretty big chip on his shoulder when he came into this program. But as time went on, we could see in this man's face the change in his self-esteem.

The people in the program, in his particular class, which was our first class back in '93, were able to take up his cause, and help this man find a job.

This is a changed person. He did get a job at Lotus Development Corporation at the end of the program. But he said he is ten years older than the parents of the person that he reports to at the office.

We have asked him if his age has been a problem; he doesn't feel that it has been. And we don't think it has been.

We have found that these Fellows have had a marvelous attitude about the program. They have said to us, "Just get us in the door. We'll show these people what we can do."

And that's in fact what's happening. They're not only doing the five-month project that they've been assigned. They are taking home manuals. They are reading, doing research. They're doing everything they can to make themselves more marketable to the company, and to the industry in general.

It's really been a phenomenal experience for them, and for us watching it from the outside.

Now, I read some of the literature that's been put out by the AARP on older workers. And I read that older workers are generally rated negatively on flexibility, trainability, and acceptance of new technology.

And I just wanted you to know, from the standpoint of our program, that people in our program understand that this is a different world, and that they are going to have to change. So they've come to our program with that recognition.

We have found them to be very open to learning all kinds of new things. And obviously because we're in a technology industry, they have to come into the program with some understanding that they need to become more familiar with technology. So we have not experienced the kinds of problems that have been identified in some of your research.

Let me end with a story about one physics professor who was for many years at the Draper Laboratories in Massachusetts. He taught himself one of the up-and-coming languages, Visual Basic. He was working on a project with a very small software company. He helped that company port their programs over into Visual Basic, and they hired him.

So I'm happy to report to you that the company is doing well, and this individual is doing well. What I also need to tell you is that this individual is 73 years old.

One of the nice things that's happened to the Software Council and to the Fellowship program is that it has been touted as a national model by some people. NBC News came in to film us. They did a program on retooling the American work force about a year ago.

INSTRUCTIONS AND QUESTIONS

1. How would you label the Fellowship Program as an organization? Many lists of possible descriptors exist. For example, you could use sources such as Amitai Etzioni, *A Comparative Analysis of Complex Organizations*, rev. ed. (New York: Free Press, 1975); Henry Mintzberg, *The Structuring of Organizations* (Englewood Cliffs, NJ: Prentice Hall, 1979); Barry Bozeman, *All Organizations Are Public:*

Bridging Public and Private Organizational Theories (San Francisco: Jossey-Bass, 1987); and David Knoke and David Prensky, "What Relevance Do Organizational Theories Have for Voluntary Associations?" *Social Science Quarterly*, 65 (March 1984): 14.

2. Describe the several ways in which the Fellowship Program has developed, either by design or by adapting to the flow of events. How do you evaluate the institutional form adopted by the Fellowship Program? You might distinguish three aspects to guide description and evaluation: market niche; standing within that niche; and character or style in which Council activities are performed.

3. Select a voluntary organization in approximately the same service niche as the Fellowship Program. What, if anything, can members of your chosen organization learn from this example? What can be usefully emulated? What should be avoided?

13

Camp Robinson

Camp Robinson is a nonprofit organization with the mission of ministering to the needs of individuals and families from all economic, social and racial backgrounds, especially those who are isolated or have a disability. The camp provides medical services for the indigent, activities for senior citizens, a weekend respite camp for mentally retarded children, and summer Med-Camps for children with various handicapping conditions.

The camp is governed by a board of directors who hire the executive director. Don, the executive director, concentrates his efforts on fund raising, grant writing, and public relations. The program director, Jennie, who reports directly to Don, is responsible for running the camp, although she gives considerable discretion and flexibility to the various program coordinators to administer their own programs. The camp hires paid counselors for camping programs but also relies very heavily on volunteers to assist the counselors.

Recently, Jennie has observed a growing tension between two of her coordinators. Ann, the director of volunteers, and Randy, coordinator of the weekend respite camps, have differing views of the role volunteers should play in the camp's programs. Ann works diligently to recruit volunteers for the camp. She has special training in volunteer management and takes her job very seriously. She organizes and runs orientation sessions for volunteers, during which she gives them a tour of the camp and introduces them to the staff. Ann is enthusiastic about volunteering at Camp Robinson and tends to paint a "rosy picture" of volunteer duties. She minimizes the tough parts of dealing with the mentally retarded clientele and concentrates on the rewards and pleasures of the job. Ann takes great pride in her volunteers and wants them to have a positive, meaningful experience in volunteerism.

Randy's primary concern is carrying out his program—assuring that the weekend respite campers are taken care of properly. Randy has a master's degree in rehabilitation and is very goal-oriented with each camper. To Randy, the only concern of volunteers should be to carry out the duties to which they are assigned and for which they were recruited. Randy has little regard for whether or not volunteers enjoy their experience or even retain a desire to return as a volunteer. In his book, the needs of the clients come first.

Ann has noticed that turnover among her volunteers is very high. Some have indicated that they do not enjoy their weekend experiences because they feel unappreciated by Randy and the paid counselors. On the other hand, Randy feels that the volunteers do not work as hard as they should. He often finds them visiting among themselves rather than interacting with the campers. The paid counselors also complain that the volunteers are not helping with the campers' needs as much as they should. The volunteers seem to participate well in the fun activities, but when it comes time to assist with feeding, bathing, and bedtime, the volunteers are often hard to motivate.

Jennie senses a real problem and knows she must take some action.

INSTRUCTIONS AND QUESTIONS

1. Outline steps Jennie should take to deal with this problem.
2. Should Jennie meet with Ann and Randy separately or together? Why?
3. Discuss the major differences, if any, in motivating volunteers versus paid staff.

14

HIV and Employee Rights

Paul Johnson is the CEO of a nonprofit in a growing community of 68,000, located 14 miles from the state's largest metropolitan area. Johnson, 36, has been CEO for two years and is a graduate of the state's only accredited masters of public administration program. He considers himself a good leader who is especially adept at resolving conflicts.

Recently, David Spencer, one of Johnson's supervisors, informed Johnson that one of the agency's employees, Jesse Neighbors, has been complaining of fatigue and loss of weight and has not reported for work during the past week.

Neighbors, 38, is openly homosexual, and speculation within the department, according to Spencer, is that Neighbors has AIDS. "After all," he told Johnson, "everybody knew that the guy was gay when he hired on. When he comes down sick, it's only logical that the guys assume he has AIDS. Some of them probably won't be too thrilled about working with him when he comes back."

Johnson acknowledged that Neighbors could have contracted HIV, but suggested other possibilities. "Hell, David, the guy could have heart disease or emphysema," Johnson said. "He smokes two packs a day. There's no need to fear the worst. We'll deal with the situation when Jesse comes back to work."

Four days later, Neighbors called Johnson to tell him that he, Neighbors, had received his doctor's clearance to return to work. During the course of the conversation, Neighbors said that he has tested positive for HIV. He speculated on how this diagnosis might affect his ability to work with the other employees. Johnson said that he was more concerned about Neighbors's ability to function effectively on the job. Neighbors assured Johnson that he was physically able to perform his work but added that he might occasionally need some personal time for a doctor's appointment.

After talking to Neighbors, Johnson called the nonprofit's attorney, David Barnes, and told him about the situation without mentioning Neighbors's name. Johnson was specifically interested in how to deal with the possibility that some employees would be reluctant to work with a person they suspected of having AIDS, but he also speculated about what obligations the agency may have to its employees concerning HIV-positive workers. He specifically asked whether the agency would be liable if another employee contracted the virus while working with an HIV-positive agency employee.

Barnes told Johnson that he would have to do some research to determine how the courts had ruled in similar cases. Meanwhile, he advised the CEO to keep the knowledge of the employee's condition confidential and to meet with the employee's supervisor before the employee's return in an effort to head off speculation.

Johnson called Spencer and asked him to meet with him at 3:00 that afternoon. When the meeting began, Johnson told Spencer that Neighbors would be coming back to work the following day. "His doctor cleared him for work, and Jesse says he's okay. That's really all I can tell you. I expect your employees to treat Jesse the same as they do anybody who's returning to work after an illness. If there's any talk about refusing to work with him because they suspect he has AIDS, I want you to call me." Spencer said he'd keep Johnson apprised of the situation.

Neighbors's first day back was uneventful, but on the morning of the second day a small group of employees from the agency, led by Charlie Wetherby, came to Spencer to say that they suspected that Neighbors had AIDS and to ask for assurance that they wouldn't be assigned to work with him. Wetherby also told Spencer that he thought all the employees in the agency deserved to know if Neighbors had indeed contracted AIDS.

Spencer told Wetherby that Neighbors's medical condition was confidential and refused to guarantee that the men wouldn't have to work with Neighbors. The controversy remained unresolved when the meeting ended. Spencer then called Johnson to tell him of the potential crisis. Johnson told Spencer to schedule a meeting with Wetherby and his group that afternoon at 4:30 in Spencer's office.

INSTRUCTIONS AND QUESTIONS

1. What are Johnson's options in dealing with the possibility that Wetherby and his fellow employees will refuse to work with Neighbors?
2. Could this situation have been avoided if the agency had instituted an AIDS policy and an AIDS education program for its employees?
3. Do Neighbors's co-workers have a right to know whether he is infected with HIV? Should Neighbors tell them?
4. Is Johnson obliged to accommodate Neighbors's condition or even retain him as an employee in light of his condition?

15

The Supply Side of Volunteerism

The demand for volunteerism or a third sector continues to be strong and indeed seems to be growing. In fact, there seems to be a stronger *demand* for volunteerism today than ever before. But, what about the *supply* side? What factors motivate people to become volunteers?

To put the essential query in another way, there is much we do not know about the specifics of the supply side, but we do know enough to provide some guidance. Exhibit 15-1 lists some major forces that seem to motivate volunteerism.

Exhibit 15-1. Why People Do "Volunteer Work"[1]

- In response to vigorous recruitment efforts
- Desire to "give something back" to a system that has permitted a person to meet his or her needs
- Sense of commitment to social and political causes
- Strong motivation to serve
- Positive attitudes about self and volunteering—e.g., a sense of personal efficacy and a conviction that "we can make it happen"

[1]Based on G. Gerger (1991), *Factors explaining volunteering for organizations in general, and social welfare organizations in particular* (unpublished doctoral dissertation, Heller School of Social Welfare, Brandeis University); and D.H. Smith (1994), Determinants of voluntary association participation and volunteering: A literature review, *Nonprofit and Voluntary Sector Quarterly, 23* (Fall): 243–263.

- Need to achieve and be useful
- Need to be prominent—a leader who makes a difference

INSTRUCTIONS AND QUESTIONS

1. Individually, and in small groups, brainstorm other possible forces that motivate volunteerism.

2. You are a member of a search committee for a nonprofit agency looking for ways to increase its supply of volunteers. How can the search committee make use of the information in Exhibit 15-1?

16

Conflicts on the Human Services Coordination Team

The meeting he dreads will begin in less than an hour, so Jerry Feldman reluctantly takes out the files on Arthur Harris and Frances Carpenter for one last review.

As Director of Field Services for the nonprofit Human Services Coordination Team (HSCT) in his state, Jerry supervises both Arthur and Frances. Arthur is Northeast Regional Director, and Frances is Arthur's specialist in inner-city problems. The team's mission is to work with citizens' groups, private agencies, public agencies, and HSCT's own program divisions to designate recipients of social services and to increase citizen involvement in their delivery. A major part of that mission involves identifying individuals and groups that need specific services and assisting them in making claims on those best able to meet their needs. The team's activities are conducted in five regions, and the field staff in each region average a half-dozen professionals and two clericals. Jerry spends a lot of time on the road visiting the regional offices, which are the central units of the team.

The regional directors, like Arthur Harris, have multiple responsibilities. They develop work assignments for their subordinates and maintain communication among them so they do not work at cross-purposes. Also, they develop the strategies and priorities for headquarters, implement them in the field, evaluate staff, and make recommendations for promotions, terminations, or reassignments. Furthermore, they supervise the administrative details that arise from the constant travel of the field workers. The nature of the team's mission is such that the regional directors have to supervise their subordinates closely and given them more corrective feedback than is common in most social-service work. After all, the team's mission is coordination, and that means that its own staff should be the best coordinated of all.

Arthur Harris's file reveals that he has been working in the northeast region as a member of the team since it was authorized a year and a half earlier. The details reveal that Arthur is a real up and comer. After three years in the Army, he completed his bachelor's degree with a double major in sociology and political science. He did one year of graduate work in sociology before taking a planning position elsewhere in the department. Selected for the team because of interest and performance, Arthur receives generally good evaluations and reflects increasing interest in "street-level" administration. Arthur is among the younger employees expected to rise to positions of considerable responsibility in the department. He is white.

Frances Carpenter is quite different from Arthur. She is seven years older, has two children, has completed about two years' college credit, and is black. Her interest in street-level administration is not new. Before joining the Human Services Coordination Team at the same time Arthur did, she was a community relations specialist with the Community Action Program in Benton, which with its sister city of Fillmore constitutes the major urban center of the northeast region. Almost everyone in Benton knows Frances's name, and in the black community of about 15,000 there are few people who do not know her personally. She led a well-publicized rent strike, worked for community control of the police, and helped initiate compensatory programs for the disadvantaged in Benton County Community College. Her specialty in the northeast region is working with the black communities of Benton and Fillmore.

Jerry has found her to be capable from the start. She is the best person in the region for handling service delivery foul-ups, both because she knows the right people and because she is inventive at creating constructive responses. Evaluations of her performance during the first year are positive. Arthur Harris's predecessor as regional director was an older black man who left the job for a top position in post-release correctional services. He had known Frances for many years, and they had worked well together.

Jerry feared that some trouble might develop when he promoted Arthur Harris, even though Arthur seemed to have support from each of his co-workers. But, initially, Arthur worked out well. After a couple of months, friction developed between Frances and Arthur, who began to write that Frances was resisting direction. He even entered notes in her file that she failed to carry out an assignment that he requested her to undertake. Other notes—none part of the permanent record—indicate that Frances frequently gets into arguments with other staff members, all of whom are white. Most recently, she had missed two weekly meetings of the field staff without notice or explanation.

When Arthur told her that if she missed a third consecutive staff meeting he would consider giving her a written reprimand, Frances blew up, called him a "racist and sexist incompetent" in tones that could be heard by anyone nearby, stormed out of the office, and disappeared for a day and a half.

Frances returned to the office in a subdued manner with a signed agreement by a voluntary agency to open a day-care center in the inner city of Benton. That was a good piece of work.

But Arthur still feels he needs Jerry's intervention, and hence the scheduled meeting which Jerry has been dreading.

Frances arrives first in the regional office's conference room. Jerry asks her to have a seat. "Good to see you," he says. "I heard about your blowup with Arthur the other day and thought the three of us ought to get together. You've worked together for long enough that an incident like this is cause for concern. Do you want to talk for a few minutes before Arthur comes in, or would you rather wait?"

"Oh, I don't know," she replies. "I'm sorry I yelled and got him upset, but he's really been after me. I used to think he was understanding, but now I'm not sure. He tries hard, but he's not as grown-up as he thinks, and he's been putting on a lot of airs."

"What do you mean?" Jerry asks.

"You know, playing like he's the big boss with all these evaluations. I've worked here as long as he has, and I know my job. He should be helpful, but instead he's always trying to act superior."

"What kind of things does he do to act superior?" Jerry inquires.

"Well, you know, Mr. Feldman, like always trying to pretend he knows better than I do what's happening in Benton, like he knows the needs there. He gives me a lot of things from books and then tries to make me feel like it's my fault, not his, when they don't work."

"Like what?"

"Like the time he wanted me to get young mothers organized for prenatal care," Frances explains. "You can't change kids' habits like that. Some are 14-year-olds hardly aware of what's happening to them. I tried a little, but there are so many other things to do, it wasn't worth the effort right then. A time will come for that. If Arthur really knew the black community here in Benton, he'd understand that."

They are interrupted by a knock on the door. "Is that you, Arthur? Come on in," Jerry calls.

Arthur is a little nervous and awkward as he sits down. He smiles at Frances and then asks Jerry how things are at headquarters. After a brief reply, Jerry suggests they get down to business. "Why don't each of you tell what you think is going on? Arthur, do you want to go first?"

"Well, if that's the way you would like to proceed," Arthur offers. "I think this is a very complicated situation with a lot of elements in it."

Arthur pauses and thinks for a minute. "I respect Frances a lot, and I'm a little uneasy saying some of this because we worked together as equals before I became her supervisor."

"I have an idea," Jerry interrupts. "Why don't you talk to Frances as well as to me? After all, whatever is going on, and whatever we manage to do here today, you two are still going to have to work things out between you."

"All right," Arthur responds. "Before I became your supervisor, when the office first opened, Frances, we worked mostly on helping people caught between the cracks in social services or people getting a bureaucratic pass-me-around—you know, case kinds of things. I don't know if you have an equal around here in handling that kind of matter."

"Well," Frances says with feigned surprise, "that's the first time you have ever admitted that!"

"Hmmm," Jerry murmurs. "Continue?"

"All right," Arthur says. "You know, casework isn't all that we should be doing. Our real goal is human-services integration. I've felt that one of the reasons I was promoted, Jerry, was because you felt that I could help this region get more into programmatic activities, you know, the kinds of things where instead of helping a few people, we implement a change that will help lots of people now and into the future."

"It's been my goal to try to do that," Arthur continues. "Things like helping service-delivery agencies establish good coordinative mechanisms between city agencies or between the county and the department, for example. We shouldn't do all the coordination, we should be setting it up so other people do that. Isn't that right, Jerry?"

"That's one of the objectives. Yes, certainly," Jerry replies.

"Well, I've tried to do that since becoming regional director," Arthur says as he looks back at Frances. "For some reason—I don't know why—you've always seemed to resist that idea."

"That's not true," Frances says.

"You'll get your turn," Jerry cautions. "Go on, Arthur, and remember to tell Frances your thoughts."

"My feeling is that both your experience and your talents lead you to prefer casework," Arthur continues.

Frances looks upset.

"Wait a minute," Jerry says. "Let's try and avoid motivations and interpretations. Just describe what happened. We'll look for causes in due time."

Arthur agrees and goes on. "The first few suggestions I gave you just seemed to bounce right off and disappear, Frances. I suggested that you try to improve coordination between County Probation and the summer softball programs in Benton County. You said you didn't know anyone in the athletic programs and that they didn't work in the city. Then there was the business with developing support in the Fillmore City Council for community-based mental-health halfway houses, which nothing ever came of. I tried to talk to you about that and tried to get you to set down on paper your goals for the next six months. But you never did. Instead, you gave me a lot of excuses about how busy you were. Then you began getting into arguments a lot during the last two or three months and..."

"What do you mean, a lot?" Frances retorts. "And besides, I didn't have many arguments, just a few disagreements."

"Man, if those weren't arguments, I don't know what they were!" Arthur notes with an exaggerated shrug.

Jerry laughs. "What's an argument to you, Arthur?"

"That's kind of hard to define," he says. "I guess when people start getting heated over their disagreements."

"What about you?" Jerry asks Frances.

"Well, both people at least have to start yelling. If my ears don't hurt it's not much of an argument," she responds.

"OK," Jerry says. "What happened next?"

"I don't know," Arthur says. "Things just started to go downhill. I feel that Frances just hasn't kept up with the others in terms of program improvements. I tried to get her to see this at the weekly staff meetings by having other people talk about what they were doing."

"That was an attempt to put me down," Frances asserts.

"Hold on," Jerry says. "Let's keep motives out of it. How did you feel? That's the question."

"Well," she says, "I felt angry. He never wanted to..."

"Tell it to Arthur," Jerry reminds her.

"Man, you are something," Frances says. "All right, *you* never wanted to hear about what I was doing. I was doing a lot of things. I got the locations changed on the health clinics, and I found a way to get hot meals for the old folks, and I steered a group of kids into a teen center they never knew existed, and a whole lot of other things. But all those meetings were a lot of talk about bureaucratic I-don't-know-what. I thought I was supposed to work against that, not make more of it!"

"That's just the point," Arthur says. "If we don't make these agencies work right, then no one will get the services they need. I know you mean well, but in the long run this way is better for the black community and all the people."

"What do you know about the black community?" Frances shoots back. "Have you ever lived there? That's what I'm supposed to know. If you knew anything about the black community you'd know better what is an argument and what isn't."

"Well, when someone stomps around an office picking fights and contradicting everyone, that's an argument," Arthur says.

"Oh, you and your bourgeois standards," Frances replies. "What do you know? I have a right to get upset once in a while," she says assertively. "Besides, what am I supposed to do? There's no one in that office I can talk to. Everyone's so concerned with doing good they never bother to find out what the people are like."

"You don't have any monopoly on the people," Arthur responds. "We work with lots of different kinds of people. It's not just the black community, and you have to understand that."

"I think we are getting diverted from the main issue," Jerry proposes. "Why don't you tell Arthur more about his idea of programs?"

"Well, he's got some problems about black folks that need some work, but all right." She turns back to Arthur. "I never did understand all that program stuff. I remember about the softball leagues, but I don't know any of those people. When I came to you about that you just gave me some names to call. Well, I had already got the names! And I tried to talk to people in Fillmore, and they gave me the run-around. They're a lot of racists over there, and you never should have asked me to deal with them. Charlie Welsh knows all those people. Why don't you ask him?"

"That's just the point. You have to expand your base of operations if you are going to become programmatic," Arthur says. "You should be able to deal with all kinds of situations. If you are going to get good evaluation reports, you have to do the same as all the other field officers."

"Who's doing the evaluations? You?" Frances asks. "How are you going to evaluate me? You don't understand the black community, and you don't know our needs. I was hired to work on the things I know best," Frances states, "and that's what I do. You got all these fancy ideas about programs and all that bureaucratic stuff, but you don't understand blacks or how to evaluate us. You don't understand me enough to help me when I ask for it, so how can you evaluate me? All you do is put me down at staff meetings, then you wonder why I don't come."

"I certainly can evaluate you and your work," Arthur maintains. "I use the same standards that I use to evaluate anyone's work. There's no difference between black or white. This isn't a race issue, and I resent your trying to make it one," Arthur snaps.

"Well, that's where you're wrong," Frances responds. "If you think you just go out and hang the same standards on all people, you *are* a racist and you don't even know it!" Frances yells. "You call yourself a supervisor and think you can evaluate me? You don't even know what I do, and you don't even care. All you care about is your so-called program plans, and I don't need any of that white middle-class stuff that's been keeping black people down for years!"

INSTRUCTIONS AND QUESTIONS

You are Jerry. A welcome emergency long-distance call gets you off the hook for a few moments. You steal a few more minutes to reflect on the meeting. So far, the discussion has ventilated some issues, and things are beginning to get hot.

1. As Jerry, where would you like to see the discussion go from here?
2. How do you think you have handled the conflict so far, and what do you think you should have done differently?
3. What have you done well about directing the discussion?
4. You tick off some of the issues. Is Arthur racist? Do you think he understands the "black community"? Do you think there is such a thing? Should Frances be evaluated or otherwise treated differently from the other members of the field staff?

5. You also are aware of the differences of opinion and values between Arthur and Frances. Which are proper subjects for management concern? Should you try to help find a way toward a resolution of their conflict that helps each better understand the other's goals and needs and still is consistent with the agency's mission and the community's needs?

6. With this kind of thought in mind, what will your opening intervention be when you reenter the conference room? How do you expect Frances will respond? Arthur?

17

Right to Know?

You are Jill, the on-site training coordinator for a community service volunteer workshop, and you have a problem. You need to change the room assignment for one of the training participants quickly. There are no single rooms at all, and moving Deborah into the only available room, the one with three beds, would mean explaining to the other two trainees in that room the reason for the unexpected move.

Deborah's current roommate, Betsy, saw her applying cream to "open sores." Betsy subsequently asked Deborah what was wrong. Deborah replied that she had "chicken pox." A day later however, Deborah admitted she sort of lied to Betsy and revealed that she has been HIV-positive for three years.

Now, Betsy is very angry that her roommate lied about the situation, and she wants to move out of the room immediately. Betsy admits she has very limited knowledge of HIV and AIDS. But it is evident to you that Betsy is very fearful of "catching AIDS." She keeps repeating that she had a right to know before she was assigned to share a bedroom and bathroom with a person with HIV or AIDS. Betsy confessed that she has been using a friend's bathroom down the hall because she is afraid of catching Deborah's disease. As Betsy left your office, she shouted that she would not eat at the center for the rest of the training.

Community service volunteer training sessions are designed for four days and three nights. Participants are assigned two per room in a dormitory-type facility and share bathing facilities. The majority of the volunteer trainees do not know each other before they arrive at the training and are assigned roommates randomly. Most prior situations have been handled quietly, with no outwardly visible problems upsetting the participants or interfering with the training itself. This situation is different, however.

INSTRUCTIONS AND QUESTIONS

1. You are Jill, the on-site training coordinator responsible for the housing arrangements. What will you do in the immediate situation?

2. Taking a longer view of things, what policies and procedures can be set in place to avoid similar situations in the future?

18

ACLU v. Tyler County

The documents that follow represent the contents that have piled up in the "in-basket" of David Flint. He has instructed you, his administrative assistant, to respond to all of the items. He gives only minimal guidance, then asks for "full speed ahead."

Good luck as you take on what is for you a welcome assignment of some scope and responsibility. You have been complaining about only getting "Mickey Mouse" assignments up till now.

12TH CIRCUIT COURT OF APPEALS
UNITED STATES OF AMERICA

November 1

Greetings:

Pursuant to recent rulings by this Court, and in agreement with the accord between parties to *American Civil Liberties Union v. Tyler County*, we hereby determine that the Tyler County office of the state Department of Human Services (DHS) must, in all good faith and expeditious action, (1) negotiate an equitable settlement with appropriate parties, and (2) make plans and carry out a strategy to deliver the following services:

1. Convenient and prompt issuance of federally sponsored food stamps.
2. Regular and timely distribution of surplus food products.
3. Fair treatment to all residents concerning government-subsidized housing.
4. Access to job training and employment services.
5. Provision of support furnishings such as excess clothes, furniture, foodstuffs.
6. Availability of family and individual counseling.
7. Access to transportation services in both urban and rural areas.
8. Inexpensive and comprehensive health services to include both primary and secondary medical care and preventive (wellness) programs.

Further, we instruct the administrator of the Tyler County DHS office to report quarterly to his/her superiors at the state DHS office concerning progress in these actions and for the state administrator to inform this Court of said progress on an annual basis.

Signed this _1st_ day of ___November___.

Bridget Ryan
Bridget Ryan, Presiding Judge

PEOPLE HELPING PEOPLE
Department of Human Services
Tyler County

Memo to: All Department Heads
From: José Espinosa
Subject: Determination letter from U.S. 12th Circuit Court of Appeals
Date: November 3

By now you have all had a chance to read the letter from the Court directing us to work with service providers in our area to guarantee social services to eligible recipients in this county. I have just gotten off the phone with state DHS director Bill Knight, who has emphasized the importance of our abiding by the court's determination and the settlement in the case referred to in the Court's letter. I certainly second his concern and direct you to work together with welfare rights groups, unions, citizens, elected officials, and relevant nonprofits in the county to make this happen.

Specifically, I am assigning Delphinia Wharton, Director of Case Management, to lead this effort. She will be in touch with each one of you about actions to be taken.

Note to Delphinia: Thanks for your willingness to take on this job. I am relieving you of all internal responsibilities so that you can concentrate on this project. — José

UNITED WAY OF TYLER COUNTY

Memo to: Stephen Nix, Planning Director
From: Elizabeth Walker, Director and CEO
Subject: Collaboration with DHS
Date: November 4

Steve, I just got off the phone with Delphinia Wharton over at DHS. I know you've worked with her on other projects. She is in a panic. She has just been handed a huge assignment by Mr. Espinosa—something about carrying out court orders that came out of the ACLU case of last year. Why don't you give her a call and see how we can help? You may want to talk with some of our agency directors, especially Red Cross, Food Bank, Family and Children Services, and Meals on Wheels, to get their input and cooperation. This is going to be a big one, and we'll need to crank up our network of service providers all across the county.

AMERICAN RED CROSS
Tyler County

Memo to: Varena Stalker, Director
           Division of Health and Human Services
From: Elliott Levy, Chapter Manager
Subject: Comprehensive Services Project in Tyler County
Date: November 7

Vee, Steve Nix just called to tell me about the DHS project of pulling together social service agencies across the county to satisfy the court ruling in *ACLU v. Tyler County*. Sounds like a big project that will need to include every agency that has anything to do with health and human services. Also, he said Delphinia Wharton over at DHS was asked to direct the project. She's fairly new to the county, so she'll need some help. Have any ideas?

From the Desk of Varena Stalker...

Elliott: Here's what I'd do.

1. Since Delphinia is relatively new to Tyler County, she should call David Flint over at Tyler Tech (967-9972) to get his help in pulling together this group of agencies. I've worked with him a lot and he's good. He has done a lot of this kind of collaboration and could facilitate the work.
2. She should get in touch with Jenny Gauld at the Nonprofit Center (934-8146), who has done some negotiating work. That's not her main job, but she is sharp and a quick learner. She may be able to help with the clients and other recipient groups.
3. Has anyone called the county manager? He's sharp, even though he's pretty busy keeping the county commissioners out of trouble. Local government ought to be brought in, both for their resources and political clout with state agencies.
4. Don't let Delphinia go off half-cocked. This will take some planning.
5. And, finally (between you and me), watch out for the folks over at United Way. They'll try to take over the whole show if you let them.

TYLER COUNTY COMMISSION
Keeping Tyler County Green for Its Citizens
Office of the Manager

November 14

Ms. Delphinia Wharton, Director
Division of Case Management
Tyler County Department of Human Services

Dear Ms. Wharton:

I have not had the pleasure of meeting you yet, but want to welcome you to Tyler County. We here in the courthouse are eager to help you in any way possible.

To that end, I understand that you have been entrusted with the task of carrying out the directives of the 12th Circuit Court of Appeals concerning the ACLU social services case of last year. We are sympathetic with the enormity of that task and pledge our resources if we can be of service.

Perhaps you would want to hold your meetings here in the courthouse. We could provide you with refreshments and a part-time secretary if that would help.

Please call me and tell me how I can assist you. Prompt resolution of this case is in all of our interests.

Sincerely,

Bill Donald

Bill Donald
County Manager

Phone message

To: Dr. Flint   Date: 11/19   Time: 1:15 P.M.
Ms. Delphinia Wharton at DHS telephoned (569-3211). She wants to talk to you about your helping on a collaborative effort.
DWS

(Confidential memo for file)   David Flint

11/19

Returned call from a Delphinia Wharton. We talked in detail about my helping her on collaborative effort related to ACLU decision from Court of Appeals. She said she was calling Jenny Gauld and wanted my advice. I told her Jenny is first-rate. D. will get back to me.

11/20

Talked with Jenny today. We agreed to help Delphinia Wharton with two-pronged strategy to negotiate a "treaty" with plaintiffs and clients and to try to collaborate with other stakeholders who will be asked to help deliver services and provide information and referral. Jenny excited about project, but in time crunch as I am. I offered my assistant as backup.

11/22

Met with Jenny and Delphinia today. D. is sharp but inexperienced. She'll do fine, but will need our assistance and advice. Agreed that Jenny would lead negotiation and I would help put together public-private-nonprofit partnership. We will propose strategy for both and we'll fine-tune. On tight timeline so will ask my assistant to turn in proposal by 12/6.

INSTRUCTIONS AND QUESTIONS

1. You are Dr. David Flint's assistant, and he hands you the file with the items present above. Develop a preliminary plan of action to assist Delphinia Wharton. Where are the potential minefields? What other information do you need, and from whom, as you move toward developing the proposal requested by Dr. Flint?

2. What is the strategy for ensuring collaboration, if any, underlying your preliminary plan?

19

After All, Nobody Got Hurt!

Bonnie D'Angelo slams the door of her downtown building and steps back to survey its two-story facade. "I ought to get rid of this white elephant," she mutters to herself. "After all, I'm not making any money on it. Nobody wants to rent a 50-year-old building. I'll be lucky if someone wants to buy it for anything close to what it's worth."

Bonnie has been a successful businesswoman for the past 20 years. She has bought and sold several businesses, watched her investments grow, and now she is ready to settle into semi-retirement and live off her dividends and rental properties. If she can just get rid of this last piece of property, she will reduce considerably her tax load and take it easy.

Across town in a small storefront office, Oscar Williams stares at the wall across from his desk, a wall badly in need of some patching and new paint. As director of the city's RSVP (Retired Seniors Volunteer Program) agency, Oscar wants to move the program's offices to better quarters, but he feels that he doesn't have the money to rent or buy the space he really needs.

Through a mutual friend, Bonnie and Oscar meet at a reception shortly thereafter. After just five minutes of conversation, they realize they might be able to solve each other's problems. When they meet at Bonnie's vacant building the following Monday, Oscar knows immediately that he wants to move in. But how can he afford the rent? He certainly doesn't have the funds to buy the building.

Bonnie offers a solution: "My holding company will rent it to you for a dollar a year and you can pay me personally an amount equivalent to the taxes on the building. That should save you a lot of money and give me a good tax writeoff as a charitable donation."

Oscar ponders the plan, asking himself, "Can I do this, ethically and legally?"

INSTRUCTIONS AND QUESTIONS

1. Can Oscar do as Bonnie suggests, ethically and legally?
2. What ethical principles come into question?
3. What alternative plan(s) would you propose?

20

An Unwelcome Advance

Jennifer Martin began working as an attorney for the local chapter of the ACLU soon after her graduation from law school. She found the job challenging, got along well with most of her colleagues, and seemed likely to advance quickly.

But the actions of a fellow attorney, Clint Harrison, often troubled her. When she encountered him in the corridors and they engaged in conversation, he stared at her breasts. On other occasions he'd stop at her office door and linger for a minute or two until Martin asked him what he wanted. Harrison's response was usually something like, "Oh, nothing. I was just admiring your beautiful hair."

Martin soon began avoiding Harrison as much as possible, but some daily contact was inevitable because of office proximity and their professional relationship; they had recently been assigned to work on a case with two other attorneys. The group met twice a week, and Harrison's presence at the meetings made Martin apprehensive. She considered asking her supervisor to excuse her from the case, but she was reluctant to explain the reason for such a request.

Late one Friday afternoon, Martin got a call from Harrison asking if he could see her in his office to talk about the case. Reluctantly, Martin agreed. She walked the short distance to Harrison's office, put on her best professional demeanor, and knocked on the door.

"Hello, Jenny, come on in and have a seat," Harrison said.

"You wanted to see me?" she asked, as she stepped into the office. Harrison took Martin's arm and ushered her to a chair across from his desk. As she sat down, she felt his hand on her shoulder. Harrison then began stroking her neck and rubbing her shoulders with both hands. "Jeez, you're tense," Harrison said. "You're going to have to lighten up, quit working so hard."

"Please don't do that," Martin said, making an attempt to get out of the chair.

"Okay," Harrison said, raising his hands. "Just trying to put you at ease. I don't like to see somebody as pretty as you under so much strain. Sit back down and let's talk."

"What did you call me in for?" Martin asked.

"Oh, I've got a couple of questions about the Hutchinson case."

"What questions?" Martin said. "I thought we'd covered everything during our last meeting. I don't see any point in talking about it until we meet again. We've all got our assignments. Now if you don't mind, I'm going back to my office. And I'd appreciate it if you wouldn't bother me anymore."

Martin rose and abruptly left. Just down the hall, she met Martha Connell, a paralegal, who noticed that Martin was upset.

"Is something wrong, Jennifer?" Connell asked. "You look really mad."

Martin clenched her teeth. "It's nothing. Just a misunderstanding. I got it worked out."

"You were in Harrison's office, weren't you? Has that jerk been bothering you? I wouldn't be surprised. He's done it before. Somebody ought to report that guy."

"It was nothing, Martha. I can handle it," Martin said. "I know how to deal with guys like him."

"Well, you shouldn't let him get away with it. You don't have to take that kind of crap from somebody you work with. He's a lawyer, for heaven's sake. He ought to know better. And I'm telling you, you're not the first one. He's made advances toward most of the pretty young women here. And he stares at—no, he *ogles*—all of them. He's a pig!"

"It's not a big deal," Martin repeated. "If he gives me any more trouble, I'll tell Mr. Hume. But I don't think he'll bother me anymore. I made it clear that I didn't appreciate his attitude. He'll leave me alone now, I'm sure."

INSTRUCTIONS AND QUESTIONS

1. Do you consider Harrison's behavior sexual harassment?
2. Should Martin have asked to be exempted from working with Harrison? If she had decided to make such a request, should she have been candid about her reasons?
3. Should the ACLU and other local nonprofits or voluntary organizations conduct seminars or meetings for employees to make them aware of what constitutes sexual harassment? Why? Sketch the design of such a seminar or workshop, if you see it as desirable.
4. If Harrison has committed similar offenses with other women, does Martin have an obligation to file a complaint, either with her supervisor or EEOC? Consult the applicable laws for your locality.

21

Anna Lieberman, Deceased

Alan Buchner has been combating discrimination for many years, and the recent death of Anna Lieberman again forces him to confront his own values and to decide what he should do. He reviews, painfully, his history and that of Anna.

A veteran of civil-rights marches from the earliest days, Buchner was interested in the plight of the elderly years before it became fashionable. He held a number of responsible positions in the social-service agencies of his community, most recently as director of an extended-care facility that was recognized around the state for its innovative programming. Buchner was active in professional societies and in meetings of "concerned citizens." He organized, and still chairs, a leading local citizen-advocate group for the elderly. Although regarded by his friends and followers as dedicated, professional, efficient, and extremely competent, he is criticized by those less fond of him. His critics find Buchner ideological, often tactless though effective, and generally involved in too many projects to do justice to all of them. Buchner recently was hired as the director of an experimental program for the mentally retarded, which is financed by a local foundation.

Local community care for the retarded is not well financed. There is sufficient local and state funding for institutionally maintaining dependent people, but there is little left for either clinical or vocational programs. Buchner was hopeful that if his program showed some success, it might open the door for better funding of similar experiments and perhaps even change community attitudes toward the elderly and retarded.

Buchner's new job involves managing a halfway house for retarded adults who have been institutionalized for many years. If such people can be brought more into community life, Buchner reasoned, then other institutionalized people might later get a similar opportunity. In a halfway house, there are only two or three people to a room. These "clients" can leave the house with freedom, go out to shop, or go for a walk. Clients get closer, more personal attention in a halfway house than in a regular mental institution where the "patients" or even "inmates" are often kept in large wards with many beds, eat institutional food at long tables, and, during the day, sit in the "day room" attached to their ward when not receiving some kind of treatment.

Buchner's halfway house employs several unit leaders, each of whom works with several client groups. A client group is composed of two to four clients plus an equal number of therapy aides and service coordinators. In addition, there is a staff of advocates who are supposed to protect the rights of the clients with respect to professional treatment, in client dealings with other members of the staff of the halfway house, and in their relationships with people outside the halfway house.

Buchner is able to recruit a dedicated staff composed largely of people who came to know him in his previous professional or community activities. But, one problem Buchner has not been able to solve is that of providing medical services for the clients. The halfway house needs a contractual, prepaid group arrangement for medical services that will assure comprehensive and timely care of the clients' needs.

Buchner's successes and failures are both patent in the case of Anna Lieberman. Anna came to the halfway house after virtually a lifetime spent in institutional settings. She had first been placed in a private institution for children at the age of 3. Anna's parents died when she was 15. Anna's older sister was her closest friend, and she cared for Anna and financially supported her. But when Anna was 25, her sister was killed in an automobile accident. Under the management of the state, Anna's inheritance from her sister lasted only two years. At age 27, Anna was moved from the private children's facility into a state institution. Two years later, she was accused of having sexual relations with a male client at the institution. After being involuntarily sterilized, Anna was confined in a locked ward for the severely retarded and multiply handicapped. The 60 beds in the ward were so close together that Anna had to climb over five beds just to get to her own.

Upon returning to her original ward after two years, Anna was emotionally withdrawn and passive. She spent most of her time sitting in a chair against the wall, staring into space. The only major variation was when her only friend, another client, came to sit and talk with her. In this institution, no one left the sitting room unless accompanied by an attendant. The ward itself included only 25 beds, reasonably spaced, and was therefore an improvement over the locked ward in which Anna was kept for two years. Formal education was never provided for Anna.

At age 59, Anna was moved again, at state initiative, to participate in an experimental project aimed at "deinstitutionalizing" those who had lived in an institutional setting for extended periods. Although she had to leave her friend, only the second she had ever made, Anna's new placement had major advantages.

Anna shared a bath with one other client and a kitchen with several others. She was given a thorough evaluation, from which it was concluded that the 59-year-old Anna was functioning at a 9-year-old level and tested at a 12-year-old level. Anna was compliant and was considered to be badly atrophied socially. This was not surprising to the staff at the new institution, for they had seen many cases in which clients suffered impairment of their ability to function even though their intellectual performance remained stable.

The staff developed a progress and treatment plan for Anna, the aim of which was to help Anna help herself in her own development. It took Anna more than a year and a half to adjust to her new environment. Her previous history made it difficult for her to respond in this strange new setting where neither corporal punishment nor behavior-modifying drugs nor restraining devices were employed routinely.

At the halfway house to which Anna was next transferred when the staff considered her ready, she made slow but continuous progress. She accepted her new independence, assumed more personal responsibility, and demonstrated less hesitancy in initiating actions. The halfway house was small enough, and Alan Buchner's hours were long enough, for him to become well acquainted with the clients. Anna developed a friendship with Alan and with Kathy Ammons, her advocate. Buchner dug into Anna's history and discovered the details of the conditions in which she had lived for so long. Kathy Ammons and Anna took a liking to each other immediately and soon developed a feeling of trust for each other.

Since Anna was older than 60 and one of the oldest clients in the halfway house, Kathy paid close attention to Anna's health. Kathy fought for regular examinations for Anna and, when indicated, for proper treatment of her friend's ills.

One Tuesday evening in December, while Kathy was visiting, Anna complained of feeling hot and having a pain in her stomach. Kathy immediately took her to the emergency room at the nearest hospital. It took three and a half hours of waiting and a heated argument before Anna was seen by a physician. He took her temperature, checked her blood pressure, prescribed a laxative, and released her. Kathy tried unsuccessfully to have her admitted to the hospital.

On Wednesday morning, Anna felt no better. Kathy went to Alan and told him of the previous evening's events. Together they were able to get Anna admitted to the hospital late Wednesday afternoon. She was placed under the care of Dr. Stevenson, one of several physicians sharing responsibilities for "charity patients." Dr. Stevenson enjoyed a community-wide reputation as a surgeon and had the political advantage of having a brother in elective state office. Although Anna had lost fluids as a result of vomiting and the laxatives, Dr. Stevenson did not start treatment to replace these fluids. He gave Anna aspirin, which stabilized her temperature at 102 degrees, but prescribed no other medication. Her situation, although not improving, was not obviously deteriorating.

On Friday morning, Buchner attended an out-of-town meeting after stopping at the hospital to see Anna. Two hours after he had

departed, she went into a coma. Kathy spent most of the day trying to reach Buchner.

Dr. Stevenson continued his treatment and responded to
Kathy's doubts with a reaffirmation of his diagnosis that Anna
was suffering from an intestinal blockage that soon would
clear up.

Buchner returned Saturday evening, picked up Kathy on his
way from the airport, and they went directly to the hospital to
see Anna. The nurse on duty told them that Anna's condition was
stable, though she remained in a coma.

Early Sunday morning, Anna died. The autopsy report stated
that the primary cause of death was a massive infection result-
ing from a ruptured appendix and compounded by dehydration.

After reading the autopsy report, Buchner sought out Dr.
Stevenson at the hospital. "Why wasn't she given fluids? Why
wasn't her illness diagnosed properly? This woman never should
have died for these reasons," he charged.

Stevenson seemed annoyed but answered calmly. "Mr. Buchner, as a physician my concern is with patients who have a future. This patient hardly had a past, let alone a future. Every day
I treat patients who have productive lives that are interrupted by
illness, and every day I know that somewhere there is the life of a
productive, contributing person that I might have saved if the
day were an hour longer. I have no time for the losers.

"You call yourself an advocate," Stevenson continued. "Why
don't you go out and advocate for the lives of the winners who
need care? I think sometimes that people like yourself are as much
losers as the pitiful beings you preserve."

Buchner could not contain his anger and snarled: "Do you realize that this autopsy report alone is probable grounds for mal-
practice? I won't stoop to discuss the ethics of that charming
speech you just gave."

"I don't think you could find a medical board or a court in
this state that would let that hold up," Stevenson retorted. A trace
of a smile crossed his face. "Perhaps you have forgotten who I
am?"

"The question is more *what* you are," Buchner snapped and
abruptly left.

INSTRUCTIONS AND QUESTIONS

Alan faces a dilemma. If he decides to initiate proceedings against the physician, Stevenson can counter with political pressure. At worst, this might jeopardize the entire halfway-house program.

Because of Stevenson's position in the medical profession, initiating proceedings probably also would decrease the likelihood of securing acceptable prepaid contractual medical services at the hospital for the residents of the halfway house.

Either outcome would be a setback for the advocates of quality care for the retarded and the elderly, as well as for the movement for deinstitutionalization that they represent.

Failure to prosecute allows Stevenson to continue practicing his brand of medicine to the likely detriment of other patients like Anna. It also may be read as tacit support for that kind of care by other physicians with similar views. Failure to prosecute also implies serious moral issues for Buchner.

You are Buchner:

1. What will you do about the death of Anna Lieberman?
2. Now think about the case as one of interorganizational relations. What are the characteristics of the relations between the hospital and the halfway house?
3. Can you come up with a strategy that Buchner can pursue for developing a relationship with the hospital that would better meet the needs of the clients of the halfway house?

22

For Better or Worse

Practically everyone in the executive staff at the Philadelphia regional office of a national voluntary agency is shocked by the
news. Bill Evans, an acknowledged contender for the assistant
director's position, has sent in his letter of resignation. It arrived,
without warning, by registered mail on Monday, February 7. By
Wednesday, Bill has not dropped by the office to explain. His personal effects are still scattered throughout his desk, his galoshes
lie at the foot of his clothes tree, and the huge greeting card he
received from his staff on his 40th birthday is still gaily decorating
his credenza.

You are Bill's superior, away on an extended business trip when his
certified letter of resignation arrives. Your secretary has your standing
order to open certified letters that arrive in your absence. Somehow,
the word about the resignation gets around.

Your secretary is finally able to contact you at 9 A.M. on Tuesday.
She tells you the news and apologizes for "the word already being
out."

You do some quick backtracking on Wednesday, February 9, when
you return from the business trip.

The formal record provides some clues about Bill's action of
February 7. This was his fifth assignment for the agency. His fam-

ily had made their fourth long-distance move about seven months before when he moved to the Philadelphia office. He was in the Atlanta area for five years previously and received two solid promotions there. He has come a long way, and many have predicted he could go much higher if he wished.

A few discreet inquiries among Bill's close acquaintances in the agency provide some illuminating details. His wife and four children—ages 17, 15, 13, and almost 7—were settled deeply into their suburban community outside Atlanta and reacted poorly to the news of another possible move. Bill looked forward to his promotion but experienced very mixed feelings about leaving Atlanta. He was coach of a Little League team there, his membership in the local Catholic church was fulfilling, and he was a Big Brother to a local black youth—a relationship he wanted to maintain. Perhaps most important, his Atlanta job permitted him to spend more time with his wife and family. The Evanses lived close to Bill's office, so he spent little time commuting. In addition, no one was very concerned when Bill left work early on those days when his wife wanted him around the house.

After a considerable period of indecision, the promotion and promise of still bigger things became compelling. The Evans family left Atlanta for Philadelphia.

Things quickly went from bad to worse for the Evanses. Their youngest, a son, had the most immediate reaction. He began to experience nightmares just before leaving for Philadelphia in August. The nightmares continued for several months and intensified enough to make the boy's first full year at school a major trial for him. The nightmares became less of a problem over time, but his adjustment to school was difficult and his academic progress remained unsatisfactory. He was placed in the slowest reading group in his new school, although he had done above-average schoolwork in Atlanta.

The two oldest children, girls aged 17 and 15, also seemed to react strongly to the move. Their relationship with their mother had been uneven for several years, but suddenly it turned tempestuous. Changing high schools seemed a major factor, and both girls resented not being able to graduate with "their class." The older girl also left behind a steady boyfriend, the captain of his high school basketball team.

Bill often became the pawn in the blustery encounters between the girls and his wife. Both his daughters and his wife competitively sought to gain his good favors, and even when he succeeded in not committing himself to one side or the other, tears and pouting tended to follow. Bill felt caught in the middle.

Bill's wife, Arlene, experienced the greatest adjustment problems. At first, the excitement of buying a new, and more expensive, house kept her going. But that experience soon palled. The Evanses went in over their head for the brick house they finally settled on within commuting distance of Bill's office. It was much less house than they had owned in Atlanta, and more costly. Bill also had a 40-minute commute each way. Consequently, he would have been around the house less even if his new job had not required a lot more of his time. His new job demanded a lot of time to begin with and stayed that way. New responsibilities were continually added to his job just as he mastered the old.

Moreover, Arlene, his wife, had trouble "fitting in." The families in their new neighborhood tend to be younger. Many of the wives are college-educated and their husbands seem to make more money than Bill, or at least they live like it. Arlene is older than most of her neighbors and feels somewhat "dowdy" in comparison to the other wives. She finished high school but could not envision four years in college. She is what her Atlanta neighbors called a "good old country girl," with all the simpler virtues.

Arlene first grieved for awhile about the loss of her very satisfying neighborhood relationships in Atlanta, then aggressively sought to establish herself in her new neighborhood. Her efforts were personally unsatisfactory, although it seemed to Bill that their neighbors accepted and even liked his wife. The reasons Arlene marshaled as underlying her dissatisfaction were numerous. She considered her new neighbors aloof and distant; Arlene did not care for bridge, "the" local game, and her new neighbors sometimes poked fun at her southern accent and that of her children. Over time, an increasingly deeper depression set in.

Arlene had barely been a social drinker in Atlanta, but soon after moving to Philadelphia, her cocktail hour began to start progressively earlier and to end later. There have been several stormy encounters between Bill and his wife over the past few months about what he calls her "drinking habit." Her standard retort has been, "You have your new job; I have my new pleasure."

Matters came to a crescendo on Friday, February 4. A small dinner party had been arranged for that evening, with the Evanses for the first time planning to entertain two of Bill's close work associates and their spouses. About 3:30 that afternoon, however, Bill called home to tell his wife that he probably would be late getting home and to ask her to entertain the guests until he arrived.

"Don't hurry," she replied. "There's no dinner party tonight. Call it off. Your daughter has run away. I just found her note." Bill sensed a slurring of his wife's speech that suggested her cocktail hour had already begun.

Bill was still gathering details from his wife as he penciled a note to his secretary to cancel the dinner engagement. Their oldest girl, he learned, had skipped school that day, apparently to fly back to Atlanta for the big basketball game at her former high school. The note she had left behind was vague, but it was reasonable to surmise where she had gone and why.

Bill asked his wife to call some of their old Atlanta friends to see if they knew anything. Arlene replied: "Never! Not my friends!" then hung up abruptly.

Bill hurried through the work that kept him late that day, agitated but still controlled. His anger at his wife was growing, as was his concern about his daughter. His drive home was a little reckless.

When Bill arrived home, he found his wife in the living room, lolling on the sofa, obviously well into her "new pleasure." Two of the children were in their bedrooms, sobbing softly.

Before the weekend was over, Bill had his letter of resignation in the mail.

INSTRUCTIONS AND QUESTIONS

1. It is now late Wednesday afternoon. As Bill's superior, what short-run course of action will you take?
2. Consider agency policies or procedures that might decrease the probability of similar occurrences in the future.
3. Does your agency bear some responsibility for Bill Evans's misfortune? Do you?

23

Taking Risks for a Good Cause

Cora Berry, director of the county's RSVP agency (Retired Seniors Volunteer Program), didn't hear John Drew, one of her board members, enter her office. Even after he called her name, she didn't immediately respond. Cora was deep in thought about a troubling issue that had come up in that morning's board meeting. John had questioned her method of documenting volunteer time and in-kind contributions of the volunteer stations. Now he had come by to discuss his concerns further.

John began, "Cora, I know you have the best interests of the agency in mind, but I'm afraid the auditors are going to detect our little deception about in-kind contributions. We've got to cover ourselves with authentic documentation."

"John," Cora said wearily, "in theory I agree with you." She added: "All of the 30 volunteer stations are supposed to send us a monthly record of the time our volunteers serve and the free lunches and other services they provide them. But they just don't do it. I'm lucky if half of them get their paperwork in on time and in the correct fashion. I know they're providing ample in-kind contributions for us to meet our 30 percent match from local sources. They tell me so when we talk on the phone."

"I don't care what you know, it's what they document that counts," John shot back. "As a board member, I don't want to take the risk of losing our funding. And another thing—while we're talking about taking risks, when are we going to get liability insurance for the board of directors?"

Cora responded, "John, we've discussed this before. You know how much liability insurance costs. We simply can't afford it."

"Well, in that case, I resign," John said, as he headed for the door.

INSTRUCTIONS AND QUESTIONS

1. Is John being realistic? Does he have a legitimate concern?
2. What should Cora do?
3. Effective risk management requires adapting general procedures to the organization's specific circumstances. What are the major steps in the risk management process?
4. State laws vary greatly in their approach to nonprofit liability. What is the law in your state regarding the legal liability of nonprofit board members? Of volunteers?

24

The Diverse Meanings of Diversity

"Diversity" has become a buzzword nowadays, perhaps nowhere more so than in the world's burgeoning nonprofit sector. Diversity is mentioned in relation to employees, clients, stakeholders, financial supporters, competitors for scarce dollars, and so on.

We often think of "diversity" in terms of gender, race, and culture, but these distinctions are only some of the differentiating features that have been considered relevant. Others include sexual orientation, pervasive differences in opinions, specific life experiences such as having been sexually harassed or molested, and so on through a very long list. Interpretations of "diversity" vary widely, and organizations differ greatly in their treatment of people with varied backgrounds.

Historically, responses to diversity in the United States have gone through a series of stages. These stages are listed below. Complicating the process, later stages often have induced conceptual confusion because earlier stages did not just wither away.

STAGES OF RESPONSE TO DIVERSITY

Stage 1. Diversity Under Duress

The answers to the following questions may surprise you:

- Which one of our major military services was the first to include 20 percent African-Americans?
- When did the first African-American attend West Point, one of our military service academies?

Answers: the U.S. Calvary and 1870, respectively. Were you, the reader, as incorrect as many people? For details, see the tragic history of the Buffalo Soldiers in the U.S. Cavalry during the decades immediately following the Civil War (Leckie, 1967). Following a nasty war between the states, the Cavalry was faced with the task of "pacifying" the western U.S. territories. Racist qualms were overcome on the grounds of expediency. Military leaders reasoned that given the incredible casualty rates in the Civil War and the rugged western conditions, it was more realistic to allow African-Americans the opportunity to serve (and often suffer or die) than to hope for sufficient enlistments by whites, because white enlistment had declined precipitously as the Civil War wore on.

Despite the sacrifices made by African-American soldiers, however, racism had only a temporary dent put in it. During the decades following the Civil War, privations and humiliations for African-American soldiers continued even as they served dutifully and often with distinction. Illustrations of the inhumane treatment abound. For example, regulations specified a *minimum* distance between African-American and white soldiers—about 50 feet.

No sooner was the "pacification" of the western territories accomplished than the military returned to its previous exclusionary policies. One clear sign: the first three African-Americans were enrolled at West Point between 1870 and 1890, but the fourth was not admitted until 1945, half a century later (see also Marszalek, 1994).

Stage 2. Diversity as Equal Employment Opportunity

Diversity reappeared in other conceptual clothes during the early 1940s. This stage can be characterized as attempts at "leveling the playing field." Basically, World War II required the contributions of Americans of all colors, races, and genders, and a booming postwar economy encouraged a corresponding sense of fairness. The prevailing attitude was that everyone should have an equal shot at qualifying for available jobs—hence, "full employment" along with the extension of educational and training opportunities to veterans of all races by the GI Bill of Rights.

What were the major limitations of this push for greater fairness, whetted by good times? Well, not much diversity resulted, with the exception of the military. Moreover, the slim gains achieved usually were concentrated in entry-level jobs. Equal opportunity, or "leveling the playing field," did not work quickly or thoroughly (Golembiewski, 1995).

Stage 3. Diversity as Affirmative Action

The shortcomings of "leveling the playing field" led to significant pressures beginning in the 1960s to "tilt the playing field." This stage attempted to make American organizations "look more like the country" by utilizing employment "targets" and "quotas" for specific populations. A spurt in honoring diversity in employment did occur, but it was uneven across "protected classes"; moreover, only modest changes occurred at middle and senior management levels.

Moreover, this stage witnessed many signs of a return to diversity under duress, with the courts often providing the defenses against reactionary backlashes. Resistance to affirmative action grew, especially in connection with "quotas" or "targets" that were widely seen as conflicting with meritocratic principles. To many, striving for "equal outcomes" went too far beyond allowing "equal opportunities." Indeed, many saw "quotas" as in basic conflict with equal access and fairness.

Problems with affirmative action suggested that enforced changes in corporate demographics were insufficient to achieve productive and diverse organizations at all levels. Judicial coercion seemed necessary but insufficient to induce full-fledged diversity in the workplace.

Stage 4. Diversity as Valuing Differences

Many came to see that major steps toward "valuing differences" would be necessary to promote cooperation and productivity within an increasingly diverse work force. Central in this insight was the sudden agreement among demographers in the late 1980s that the changes in workplace composition had just begun. Many observers concluded that the challenges in rectifying the errors of the past would be exacerbated by predictable demographic changes in the American work force over the next decade or two. White males would find themselves in the minority. After 2005 or so, for example, respected demographers estimated that 40 percent of new American employees would be non-Caucasian.

Hence the sudden profusion of diversity workshops and other ways to help workers understand differences, in the hope that understanding would lead to valuing, and that in turn greater valuing would trigger changes in attitudes and behavior. Estimates are very tricky here, but millions of employees no doubt had one dose or another of training programs designed to promote understanding of diversity.

The intent was clear enough, in any case. The purpose was to induce a more receptive context for progress toward diversity. This approach was, in effect, a "bottom up" counterpart to the courts' "top down" enforcement measures.

Although well intentioned, efforts directed toward valuing diversity have had serious shortcomings. For one thing, the training programs seldom involve intact work teams, or—to say much the same thing in a different way—diversity training had an intrapersonal emphasis. Even the more meaningful programs had limited long-term usefulness. Transfer of learning to worksites and large systems was incomplete, and the internal dynamics of organizations were seldom affected.

Stage 5. Managing Diversity

Today, a growing awareness of the limitations of previous approaches leads to the conclusion that change in organizational features—in strategies, structures, policies, and procedures—will be necessary to achieve lasting change of any kind. This awareness leads to efforts to manage diversity—to build a recognition of diversity into policies, procedures, and into the very structure of work itself (Golembiewski, 1995). Indeed, in the absence of numerous reinforcing managerial changes at multiple sites, a backlash may very well occur in response to implementation of stages 2, 3, or 4. Given a worst-case scenario, we may slide back to the first phase, or even to pre-diversity times. Thus, those who put their full faith in affirmative action will find that presidential administrations, courts, and legislatures can and do coerce change, but administrations and policies also may change. If stage 5 is neglected, managements will find it attractive to reverse pro-diversity initiatives, especially when money is tight. Those committed only to diversity under duress always will be ready to lead both political and management repression and regression.

INSTRUCTIONS AND QUESTIONS

1. Choose a voluntary or nonprofit organization, either one that you know about firsthand or one you can learn about via reading or interviews. Identify the approach to diversity that seems to characterize your target organization. Perhaps you may see different approaches implemented in several policy arenas or functional areas.
2. Do you observe any contrasts or contradictions—e.g., disjoints between official policies concerning diversity and day-to-day practices within your target organization?

References

Golembiewski, R.T. (1995). *Managing diversity in organizations.* Tuscaloosa, AL: University of Alabama Press.

Leckie, W.H. (1967). *The Buffalo Soldiers.* Norman, OK: University of Oklahoma Press.

Marszalek, J.F. (1994). *Assault at West Point: An account of the ordeal of a black cadet.* New York: Collier Books.

25

The Homeless Just Need a Fighting Chance

Sharon Meyer is a nurse-practitioner who delivers primary medical care to the homeless population in a city of 280,000 people for a nonprofit outpatient health clinic. Each weekday morning at 6:00, she fires up the van parked behind the health clinic and begins making the rounds of four downtown shelters. In recent weeks, she has added stops at the railroad yard, the warm-air sidewalk grates next to a bank, and the corner where homeless men wait for day work. Although her mobile clinic is well equipped, she is hesitant to diagnose and treat serious problems, especially those dealing with respiratory illness and communicable diseases. She prefers to refer people with serious symptoms to Ridgefield, the indigent-care hospital located downtown.

Recently, however, Ridgefield's administrator, whom Meyer has never liked, has enforced a limit of one homeless patient per day. "We can't afford to take in more than that," he lamented.

"We have three or four serious cases a day," Meyer complained to Karen Evans, her executive director. "How are we ever going to help these people if Ridgefield Hospital won't accept more than one homeless patient per day?"

"You're absolutely right," Evans replied. "We're also having trouble with the local homeless shelters. They don't always take our referrals."

Together, the two health care advocates hatched a plan. They decided that they would provide fictitious home addresses for the additional homeless people requiring treatment at the hospital, hence qualifying them for free medical care and circumventing the administrator's ban. They also agreed that they would start spreading the word that local shelter managers are discriminating against the homeless with health problems.

Meyer and Evans both recognize that they need Ridgefield Hospital and all the shelter managers to be team players in their fight against homelessness in the city. They also feel frustrated in their efforts to secure adequate medical care and shelter for their homeless clientele with serious health problems.

INSTRUCTIONS AND QUESTIONS

1. What are the likely "unintended" consequences of Meyer's and Evans's plan regarding Ridgefield Hospital and the shelters?
2. Design a more effective strategy for securing medical and shelter care for homeless people with health problems.

SECTION 3

Strategies for Managing and Improving Nonprofit, Voluntary, and Third-Sector Organizations

26

Changing Missions for Nonprofits

THE CENTRAL STATE LEGAL AID SOCIETY

The Central State Legal Aid Society is contemplating whether to begin charging its clients a modest fee in order to generate much-needed income. The Society's mission statement describes its primary purpose as providing free legal aid. In the past two years, the number of clients served has increased 150 percent. Unfortunately, funding has not kept pace with this rapid growth. The monies gathered through private gifts, some small grants from local foundation groups, and special work performed by the Society for the local bar association are no longer sufficient. In fact, the current budget crisis is very deep, and the organization must either cut back its total client load significantly or begin to request fees from its clients.

CARRIE NATION WOMEN'S UNIVERSITY

An all-female private college, responding to decreasing enrollments, is advised by an external consultant to consider "going co-ed" to remain competitive. Yet the majority of the faculty and alumni feel that opening the college to male students would threaten its fundamental mission of serving young women. The school has had some cooperative programs and courses with another nearby private college that is already co-ed. The courses taught there have enrolled as much as 25 percent of CNWU's students during any given semester. Current students have called for a show of "solidarity" against those who would change the school's mission.

CULTURE CITY SYMPHONY ORCHESTRA

The Culture City Symphony Orchestra, organized forty years ago to improve the quality of the musical life of its city, must decide whether to give more "pops" concerts and fewer regular subscription concerts of classical music. The programming change would assist the organization in meeting its payroll but would compromise the orchestra's mission of providing subscription concerts of classical music. The CCSO seems divided on the issue, but the current board of directors is horrified at the suggestion.

INSTRUCTIONS AND QUESTIONS

One of the keys to a strong nonprofit organization is commitment to a well-defined mission. For each of the scenarios described above, decide whether the organization should adjust its mission to move into the proposed "new area."

1. What is the likely effect on the clientele of the existing organization as well as the "new" one if the organization does adjust its mission?
2. What is the likely effect on the organizational members (paid and unpaid staff) of such a change?
3. What is the likelihood of the general mission of each organization going "unserved" if it does *not* adapt and change?
4. Finally, in all three scenarios, what would be different if the organization were a "for-profit" organization? Governmental?

27

Organization Development in the Ashfield Youth Corps[1]

BACKGROUND

The "Ashfield Youth Corps,"[2] a church-based, voluntary youth organization, was founded to strengthen community ties by involving young people in community service. Ashfield is a suburban district of a major city and, like its counterparts throughout the world, has been characterized by a high population density and accompanying social problems, such as unemployment, crime, and substance abuse.

The Youth Corps was divided into "units," according to activity. There were five major units: *welfare action,* which catered to needs such as household repairs and improvements for the poor and elderly; *visitation* of the elderly and house-bound; *entertainment* through organizing concerts and parties; *communication* within the Youth Corps by means of a weekly newsletter; and *choir,* which sang in the local church and at weddings and par-

---

[1]Based on "Process Consultation in a Voluntary Youth Organization" by D. Coghland and Gamma Donnelly-Cox, *Organization Development Journal,* 8: 1996, (1), 36–41.

[2]Not its real name.

ties. Two other units, *catering* and *transport,* were formed on an ad hoc basis according to particular needs. The ages of Youth Corps members ranged from 15 to mid-20s.

A secretary and treasurer worked with the coordinator. A weekly meeting of unit leaders and coordinator formed policy and administered the Corps. The entire Corps met every couple of months.

Corps members decided at one meeting to engage some external consultants to assess the state of the organization with a view to training. Two consultants who had done training work with other youth organizations were contacted. In preparation, the two consultants met and discussed their orientation towards the project, with a focus on the skills they would bring to the work.

PHASE 1

For the initial meeting between the consultants and representatives of the Youth Corps, the consultants devised a process for identifying training needs. This process followed the simple format of asking members:

(a)   what the Youth Corps did;
(b)   what the perceived priorities were in (a);
(c)   what the Youth Corps thought it should be doing;
and   (d)   what the perceived priorities were in (c);
then   (e)   comparing (b) and (d);
and   (f)   selecting the top two priorities in (d) with a view to identifying training needs.

The priority lists from steps (b) and (d) were posted on newsprint. Diverse activities, from firefighting to delivering a newsletter, were listed, providing the consultants with a good sense of what the Youth Corps was about—what it did. The enthusiasm of the participants for what they were doing demonstrated something of the culture of the organization.

The consultants developed a process for the next meeting, at which the Youth Corps representatives would be given five minutes to list the key issues identified in the priority lists in relation to administration, structure, sensitivity, leadership, communication, and recruitment. These issues, it was hoped, would suggest objectives on which a training design could be built. The consultants met two members of the Corps and clarified needs. Then they made a preparatory training program design, which they intended taking back to the group for consultation and involvement in developing the actual design of the training. In the meantime, recruitment for the weekend was proving difficult. It was decided that a minimum enrollment number was necessary by a certain date. When that number was not reached, the training weekend was cancelled. The consultants were informed.

Some weeks later the consultants received a letter from the coordinator informing them that, in the wake of the cancellation, there had been a surge of interest in the weekend. The cancellation had provoked a lot of questioning within the Youth Corps, directed particularly toward the commitment of some members. It was reported that the consultants' interventions had "switched on a few lights" and that there was a high level of interest in pursuing a review process. The consultants were invited to attend the weekly unit leaders' meeting. The coordinator and the unit leaders increasingly appreciated the questions the consultants were posing, particularly those centered around identifying needs and establishing priorities. Accordingly, they wanted the consultation process to continue and suggested that the consultants attend meetings of any unit that invited them. It was agreed that units should not be pressured to engage the consultants. The consultants decided to work separately in responding to invitations from units.

Over the next few months, one or the other of the two consultants met with the five major units: communications, welfare action, choir, entertainment, and visitation. Both consultants met with the coordinator. It was found that at the outset of each meeting some clarification of the role of the consultants was necessary, and the facilitative nature of the role was explained. Each session followed a similar process, one that evoked reflection on the gap between the actual Youth Corps situation and a perceived ideal, and what would be needed to bridge the gap. For instance, the members expressed their views of the ideal functioning of the Youth Corps but then had concrete difficulties with punctual attendance at meetings and getting volunteers for a particular project. A general meeting of the entire Youth Corps was held, and each unit reported on its current state and progress since the last general meeting. The consultants attended as observers. Many units referred to the consultants' visits as helpful.

The Ashfield Youth Corps was a very loosely structured organization. The coordinator consistently refused to assume the title "director," preferring to define his role in terms of coordination and facilitation. He maintained a close, personal relationship with the unit leaders. A culture of enthusiasm, commitment, and energy was created. Actual management and organizational processes were vague and subject to frequent breakdowns. While these shortfalls typically caused frustration, the organization's high levels of energy and commitment seemed sufficient to carry it through its administrative difficulties.

The consultants met to review the project and decided to recommend terminating their work for several reasons. First, it appeared from the viewpoint of the members of the Corps that the intervention was finished, or at least that the Youth Corps members were not expecting anything else. Second, the consultants saw the effect of their intervention in terms of opening up questions about the work of the Corps. The Corps would now have to take these questions further and act upon them. Both the consultants and the unit leaders thought that it was important to allow sufficient time to elapse so that any element of novelty and enthusiasm generated by the consultants' presence could wear off and the possibility of normative change could take place. Termination itself is an intervention, and the consultants judged that it was an appropriate one at this point. It was also the beginning of summer, when the Corps' work took on a more diffuse form, so it seemed appropriate for the consultants to withdraw, and if requested, resume the contract in the autumn. Accordingly, at a unit leaders' meeting, the consultants verbally reported their view of the current situation, and the contract was terminated by mutual agreement.

PHASE II

Sixteen months later a request came to the consultants to resume working with the Youth Corps. The consultants met with the co-ordinator and some Corps members to initiate a review process. The Youth Corps members were asked to express the present situation in a single phrase or word, particularly in the light of their experiences since the previous assessment. The following descriptions typified the responses: "messy," "growing," "mixed-up," "searching," "at a crossroads," "work revolving on a few," "lack of articulated philosophy." These responses were posted on newsprint.

Then Youth Corps members were invited to describe a critical incident that exemplified the descriptions and to evaluate the degree of seriousness of the underlying issues. Issues identified included low morale, unclear leadership, too much reliance on individuals in particular units, cliques, turnover of personnel, and inadequate training of new leaders.

What did the Youth Corps now expect of the consultants? Three themes emerged: providing feedback and evaluation, facilitating reflection on the vision and philosophy of the Corps, and design of a training/reflection weekend. The consultants fed back what they had heard and linked it to their view of what had emerged the previous year. The consultants agreed to run a training weekend, and work was undertaken to fix dates and location.

Over the next few months in preparation for the training, the consultants were invited to several units to facilitate their internal review and help identify needs. The consultants confronted the organizing committee on the goals for the training weekend, as it was unclear whether the format was to consist of a social weekend with a large number of participants (which in the context of the Youth Corps would be about 60), or a training weekend with a smaller number and a more focused training agenda. Issues of training design were presented by the consultants, who clearly stated their own position. If it were to be largely a social weekend, they would help plan and design it but not participate. If a training weekend were selected, they would plan and design it, hire extra staff, and facilitate it. This intervention challenged the committee to clarify its goals. The consultants designed a preliminary outline of a training weekend that focused on leadership and group skills, personal development, and organizational planning skills. These design elements were presented to the organizing committee, discussed, and approved. The weekend for about 28 leaders was designed and a team of five, including the two consultants, facilitated it. The 28 participants were a mixture of unit leaders and members who were willing and free to attend.

The training weekend focused on three areas:

1. leadership and group skills—interpersonal communication and group process, particularly leadership style, decision-making, functional roles and inter-group dynamics;
2. personal development through values clarification;
3. organizational skills—problem-solving, planning, implementation, and evaluation.

The section on organizational skills was devoted to reflection on the transfer of learning to the Youth Corps units. Working units met separately and engaged in vision-sharing, problem-solving, and action-planning strategies. These were then presented in a plenary session. The consultants contracted to carry out a follow-up visit with the Youth Corps in two months' time to help the Corps assess its progress in implementing changes.

The weekend was deemed a great success. The Youth Corps members participated very actively and received a high degree of support and affirmation from one another.

As agreed upon during the training weekend, the consultants wrote to the secretary of the Youth Corps shortly afterwards, confirming with her that a follow-up process would be activated two months later. When this time arrived, the consultants began meeting with the members of each unit, which included both participants and nonparticipants of the weekend. Three units were met. In one, only one member had been on the weekend and was not present at the meeting. The others did not realize the consultant was attending the meeting. Some developments, particularly in inter-unit cooperation, that had resulted from the weekend were reported. In another unit, where most had attended the weekend, a lot of reorganization had taken place and the action-plans were in operation. In the third unit, the group didn't know why the consultant was there and assumed he had called the meeting. A meeting with all the unit leaders never took place.

The consultants reflected on the progress of the review process, then wrote to the coordinator and presented the following dilemma. In their view the follow-up process had fizzled out. It was difficult to assess progress. The first reason seemed to be difference of expectations. While the unit members were saying that the consultants wanted to meet them, and wondered why, the consultants conceived their visits in terms of the contracted follow-up to the training weekend. A second reason seemed that, while the training weekend had been an occasion for achieving personal growth, building morale, deepening commitment, and strengthening friendships within the Corps, the training objectives of upgrading leadership, group process, and planning skills had not been afforded the same value. The consultants viewed their work as completed, and they proposed that the contract be terminated. Some months later a reply from the coordinating committee indicated that the process of evaluation was proving difficult and that the termination was accepted. Thus the project ended.

DISCUSSION

This case provides an example of the structural arrangements of a voluntary association. As the consultants adapted to the organizational realities of Ashfield, they could start advising on organizational skills related to administration, structure, sensitivity, leadership, communication, and recruitment. Ashfield Youth Corps is a *loosely coupled* organization: while the organization is comprised of a very standard structure of units, they are only loosely connected. The links between units are informal, and each unit can function without direct contact with the others. For the members, the emphasis is on the informal organization. The membership shared strong values regarding what Ashfield ought to do and ought to be about. This has an effect on the organizational skills needed to run Ashfield effectively.

The loosely coupled structural arrangements had implications for the process consultation. Information hadn't flowed as the consultants had expected. There appeared to be a poor transfer of formal training on the level of integration of specific mechanisms, processes, and skills. However, the benefits of loose coupling also apply to Ashfield. A loosely coupled organization has the capacity for high adaptivity (Orton and Weick, 1990). It may be particularly appropriate for a voluntary youth association in which the focus is on service delivery but there is a cyclic turnover in membership and great emphasis on social interaction and cohesion.

This case also demonstrates that the *process consultation* approach to consulting is a clinical form of research (Schein, 1987a, 1987b, 1988, 1995). A process consultation approach is built on a philosophy of helping that is grounded in client-centered values and assumptions, and follows a collaborative manner of working that empowers the client "to see, understand and act upon process events" in the client's environment in order to improve the situation as perceived by the client (Schein, 1988, p. 11). The clinical approach to research is a form of action science where the researcher and consultant roles merge in both helping the organization manage its change and generating useful knowledge of how change is managed (Schein, 1987b, 1995; Gummesson, 1991).

What did the consultants learn from their work with the Corps? As the consultants were working from the process consultation approach, the challenge was for them to adapt to the organizational realities of the Youth Corps and allow the client system to set the pace. The two consultants adapted to the reality of the Youth Corps' young persons' culture. For instance, they adapted to looseness with regard to punctuality. An arranged meeting might start half an hour later than scheduled, have less than half the group in attendance, be held in very cramped quarters, have an unclear purpose, yet exhibit a high degree of friendliness, enthusiasm, and cooperation. The consultants were given the name the "Discovery Unit" and were perceived to have become "friends" by supporting the Youth Corps and provoking reflection in a non-threatening manner. They were named as honorary members, their names were included on the register of members, and they were invited to social functions. At the same time, the consultants confronted when they judged confrontation to be appropriate. In this approach, diagnosis and intervention are inseparable. As the consultants gathered data, they were intervening in the system and learning was taking place on both sides. This experience supports Schein's reflection that process consultation is a valid form of organizational research because it studies organizations from within, and out of a helping framework learns the ways things "really are" in an organization. (Schein, 1987b, 1995).

INSTRUCTIONS AND QUESTIONS

1. What are the implications of loose coupling for the effective intervention of the consultants?
2. Should the coordinator assume the role of Youth Corps director?
3. Should the structure of the Corps be altered to allow for greater cohesion within the organization?
4. What conceptual and practical adjustments to a consulting model would be helpful in working with this form of organization?
5. What skills are required of the clinical researcher?
6. What is the value of the process consultation approach to research for the study of voluntary organizations?

References

Gummesson, E. (1991). *Qualitative methods in management research*. Newbury Park, CA: Sage.

Orton, J.D., and Weick, K.E. (1990). Loosely coupled systems: A reconceptualization. *Academy of Management Review, 15*: 203–223.

Schein, E.H. (1987a). *Process consultation* (Vol. 2: Lessons for managers and consultants). Reading, MA: Addison-Wesley.

Schein, E.H. (1987b). *The clinical perspective in fieldwork*. Newbury Park, CA: Sage.

Schein, E.H. (1988). *Process consultation* (Vol. 1: Its role in organization development) (2nd ed.). Reading, MA: Addison-Wesley.
Schein, E.H. (1995). Process consultation, action research and clinical inquiry: Are they the same? *Journal of Managerial Psychology, 10*(6): 14–19.

28

Barrytown Community Resource Center

INTRODUCTION

This article* describes a consultation in which a psychodynamic perspective leads the organization to recognize and deal with important issues required for survival and change. Barrytown Community Resource Center (BCRC) is a community development organization with a central mission of fostering social change through a process of participation and empowerment. Its intention is to operate as an open system taking in clients, working with them, and moving them back into the community with a greater sense of their own identity and an improved ability to contribute to the development of their own environment—social, economic, and political.

Over time, however, BCRC had become a closed system whose primary task was unconsciously subverted into trying to meet the dependency needs of clients and workers. This happened

---

*Adapted and reprinted with permission from David O'Brien, "From Open to Closed System: A Case in Community Development," *Organization Development Journal, 16* (Fall 1996): 16–24.

because of the extent of need that clients bring to the organization, the need of workers to be nurturing, and the anxiety generated by the difficult and complex primary task of community development.

BARRYTOWN COMMUNITY RESOURCE CENTER

Barrytown Community Resource Center (BCRC) is located in Barrytown, an area on the north periphery of the city of Dublin. Barrytown is very similar to many other communities on the edge of the city. It is about 25 years old and has a population of about 22,000 people, the vast majority of whom live in local authority housing. Many people were relocated to Barrytown from the inner city. Until recently, Barrytown did not have a strong community identity. Unemployment is exceptionally high, about three times the national average (40 to 50 percent). The community has all the attendant problems related to high unemployment: drug and alcohol abuse, vandalism, joyriding, poverty, and low educational attainment.

The number of single parents allocated houses in the area is also exceptionally high. Women, in particular, experience isolation and stress. It is mostly women who have availed themselves of the Center. Many families and individuals undergo severe deprivation, and the community as a whole experiences isolation from mainstream urban society. This is the Center's "marketplace."

BCRC was established in 1985 by the local health authority in a large eighteenth-century house that had formerly been used as a children's home. The primary task of BCRC, as stated at that time, was "to provide a front-line, preventive, community-based service for families in the Barrytown South area" in the belief that "there is a real need for services which aim to prevent the needs of families reaching crisis proportions."

A project leader, a childcare worker, and a community worker were assigned to the project. It was left to the staff to develop the organization as they saw fit. In this sense it was truly an emergent organization that was expected to build and shape itself from its experience as it grew (Mintzberg, 1979). It was central to BCRC's mission at the outset to try to encourage users to become involved in its development and to participate in decision making.

It can be noted that the statement of the primary task above does not mention community development. Instead, BCRC's mission is described in terms of providing a service to the community. But since its inception, it is clear that those working in the Center, as well as outside observers, would describe it as a community development organization—that is, an organization committed to change through a process of participation and empowerment. This was the articulated primary task of BCRC at the time of the consultation.

The organization has a budget from the local health authority of £219,000. It also raises funds from other sources for additional staff and for some of its activities. It recently benefited from a government community employment scheme that provides twenty part-time jobs in the organization. There are a large number of tutors who work in the organization on a part-time basis. In all, there are approximately one hundred people working in the center on a paid basis. The total budget is about £320,000 per annum.

Apart from those working in a paid capacity, there are a substantial number of unpaid workers—volunteers—who make a significant contribution. Their input varies from a few hours a week to almost full-time unpaid employment.

BCRC serves about 300 people per week, the vast majority of whom are women. It offers a range of services, activities, and support groups. These include day care facilities for users and workers, after-school clubs, welfare rights information, a wide range of adult education classes, a drama group, a fitness group, a building restoration group, worker support group, single parents' group, and a separated persons' group.

In all there were 14 sub-groups. They were divided into three broad categories, as indicated below: services, support, and activities (Exhibit 28-1). The overall organization was managed informally by a management committee that included the professional staff team and about ten others who had come into the Center as users and over the years had taken on different areas of responsibility. They had undergone a variety of leader-

Exhibit 28-1.   Barrytown Community Resource Center

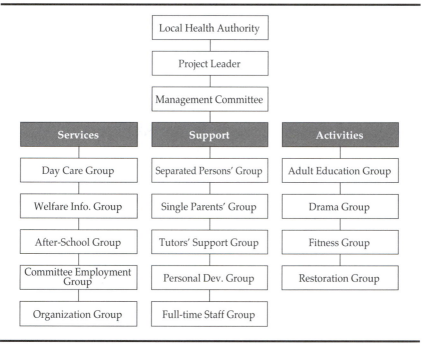

ship training programs. The committee met once a week for three hours. The committee reported to the local health authority through the project leader.

THE CONSULTATION

Overall, the structure of BCRC was not easy for an outsider to grasp. It took a number of meetings to form a complete picture. Different members of the committee were aware of different parts of the organization. No one person seemed to hold the whole organization in mind. This confusion was due in large part to the rapid growth of the organization in recent years. New needs were being identified and new sub-groups formed to address these. This confusion and lack of clarity was one of the reasons for requesting consultancy. The committee also wanted to formalize its role as management in relation to the local health authority. In order to do this, it wanted to have a clear and complete picture of the organization it was going to manage. The management committee decided to engage a consultant to help carry out a self-evaluation of all the activities in the Center.

The purposes of the management committee's self-evaluation were threefold:

1. to form a clear picture of all the activities in which the Center was engaged and their effectiveness from a users'/organizers' perspective;
2. to develop a clear direction for Barrytown Community Resource Center arising out of the self-evaluation findings; and
3. in the process, to develop a sense of its own identity as a management group.

The Steering Group

Consistent with a community development philosophy, the consultancy process itself needed to be collaborative—to be an equal partnership between client and consultant (Block, 1981; Schein, 1987). The first step in this process was to set up a steering group which would take responsibility for designing and carrying out the evaluation and feeding back the data to the committee. The steering group, in terms of its own dynamics, might also mirror some of the dynamics of the larger organization and so provide valuable insight into understanding the organization as a whole (Bion, 1969).

The steering group consisted of the consultant, the project leader, another staff member, and a voluntary member. It had been agreed with the committee that the self-evaluation would involve data gathering with all 14 sub-groups. All the sub-groups were interviewed for a half-day each. Sub-groups presented themselves in different ways. In some cases, all members of the group—both users and organizers—attended. In other cases, only the organizers presented. Each of the three "internal" members of the steering group took turns interviewing with the consultant. Data gathering took place over a five-month period.

Data and Diagnosis

The steering group met four times to analyze the data from the interviews. The following points summarize this process:

1. Each of the sub-groups had, to varying degrees, developed some form of internal management structure. In many cases, the central responsibility seemed to be firmly invested in one individual. In all cases, the sub-groups were very much attached to the Center. In fact, one group that seemed to be in a position to detach itself from the Center and to become autonomous became quite anxious when asked to look into this possibility.

2. People's personal lives were very much affected by their participation in the Center. They felt much better about themselves, learned new skills, and discovered abilities that had been latent. The Center was a central part of their lives and one which they felt they could not do without.

3. Many people belonged to several sub-groups. There was a clear sense in which the Center fulfilled many needs for individuals.

4. In relation to structure, the role of the committee was not clear to most sub-group members, apart from the project leader. Only one group, the organization group, was associated with management functions. Difficulties having to do with many aspects of day-to-day management were "dumped" into this group.

5. Leadership in its most concrete sense was located in the project leader. His responsibilities included quite a heavy counseling caseload, teaching personal development courses, and finding someone to fix the roof or deal with a security problem.

6. Perhaps the most significant point of all was the very real sense in which the Center was "full to the bursting point." This is the point that underpins the diagnosis. People from the community who were targeted by the Center because of their marginalization—being isolated for different reasons, being in difficult marital relationships, trying to raise one or more children on their own, lacking confidence because of low formal educational attainment—were encouraged to come and avail themselves of the

various programs and activities. Many came at a critical point in their lives. To them, the Center was "a lifeline," "a lifesaver," the "beginning of a new life." As they began to address needs and discover more, they came to rely on and demand that the Center devise ways to meet these needs. Instead of moving on, they stayed and continued to circulate within the Center. As a result, the Center was becoming "full" and no longer in a position to continue to take in new users. There was very little output in terms of users moving on. Moves towards independence and autonomy were absorbed into internal, slowly increasing levels of responsibility.

7. If someone did not appear for some time, the staff and other users worried about them and encouraged them to return. Leaving the BCRC was often interpreted as a sign of the Center's failure to provide sufficiently attractive programs for such people.

8. In trying to meet the developing needs of participants in the Center's programs, second- and third-stage courses had to be provided. Resources were being stretched beyond their breaking points in trying to provide for first-time users and those who wanted more advanced programs in this "safe" place.

9. Clear links with other recently developed resources in the locality had not been developed. Some of these offered similar opportunities to those being offered by BCRC.

10. The Center, while it adopted a community development approach to its work in Barrytown, was only very marginally engaged, if at all, in community development.

The Psychodynamic View

Psychodynamic theory provides a valuable and useful construct for understanding human processes in groups and organizations (Hirschorn, 1988; Bion, 1969; Czander, 1993). From the experience of being in BCRC and meeting the people involved, it seemed to the consultant that identifying certain psychodynamics of the organization provided the basis for a fruitful intervention. Other theoretical concepts, including open systems theory, emergent organization, primary task, and organizational environment, are used to understand the implications of this basic psychodynamic (Miller, 1993; Menzies, 1975, Holti, 1994a).

While acknowledging that the psychodynamics of BCRC, like that of any organization, are complex and multi-faceted, the consultant discovered one dominant feature that provided the basis for understanding what was happening: the dominant culture of BCRC was one of dependence on the Center.

BCRC is a community organization that consciously aspires to be an agent of social change through a process of empowerment. Ideally, its intention is to operate as an open system, taking in members of the local, marginalized community, working with them through an empowering process, and helping them to move beyond the Center with a greater sense of their own authority and ability to exercise it, either individually or collectively. It is believed that this process will lead to social change.

What in fact seemed to have happened was that BCRC had developed into a closed system. It took in people from the local community, helped them to articulate their needs, worked with them in response to those needs but had serious difficulty moving them beyond the Center. It had become, in fact, an almost totally closed system. This situation had developed for a number of reasons. The first was the degree of need that users brought to the Center. The Center represented a "safe" place where, perhaps for the first time in their lives, people (90 percent of them women) feel secure and cared for. As initial needs are addressed, other needs become apparent, and quite quickly the Center found itself responding to even greater nurturing demands. The process quite subtly and unconsciously slipped from encouraging empowerment to encouraging dependency. There was also an unspoken assumption that these dependency needs could actually be met. As a result of trying to respond to the increasing demands of those already using the Center, there was less and less space for new people.

The Center had become full to its "bursting point," with the same people "circulating" inside.

A second reason for this development relates to staff needs to be nurturers. The level of need of users was often so profound that it was difficult for staff not to respond; and so the more difficult empowerment agenda faded from sight (Czander, 1993).

A third reason why BCRC had developed into a closed system is that, as an emergent organization, it had not evolved structures that would have supported it as an open system. As the pressure to meet unconscious dependency needs increased, the very loose structures that evolved related more to these than to the primary task of community development. Those managing the organization were from the "inside," with no representation from other sectors and disciplines. The possibility of "outside" input, which might not get so involved in the dependency dynamic, was missing (Holti, 1994b).

A fourth reason was related to the primary task of community development—the "big agenda" of social change. Until quite recently, this agenda had been associated with confrontation and conflict. It involved engaging in struggles with the state and those in economic and political power to achieve a redistribution of resources and power. In recent times, however, a very significant change had taken place. As the state failed to find substantial solutions to the huge social and economic issue of unemployment and its attendant ills, it decided that those who had experienced its ravages might make an important contribution to its resolution. For this reason, it had made considerable funds available to community organizations and invited collaboration and partnership instead of confrontation. In light of this change in relationships, the meaning and manner of achieving the primary task of community development was no longer clear, but confusing and ambiguous. Dealing with dependency needs can be a defense against the anxiety of redefining this primary task and its potentially disturbing implications (Bion, 1969; Menzies, 1975).

In psychodynamic consulting work, it is common practice to try to gather the information into a central statement (typically called the working hypothesis) which can then be used by the organization and the consultant as the basis for further intervention (Miller, 1995). The working hypothesis in this case was that BCRC has developed from an open into a closed system for the following reasons:

1. The fulfillment by the Center of the serious dependency needs of users had become the unconscious primary task of the organization. The attempt to satisfy these needs was a defense against the overt primary task of achieving social change through a process of empowerment.

2. The emergent nature of the organization had unconsciously failed to develop structures that supported the overt primary task and established the organization as an open system.

Instead, the structures that emerged allowed the overt task to be avoided by expanding the work in ever-widening circles to respond to primary needs of dependency.

Having said all this in relation to BCRC, it is important to state that the request for consultancy was to help the organization form a clear picture of what was happening and to provide direction for an appropriate future. The Committee, with the help of the steering group, was able to analyze and begin to consider developing a culture of real empowerment that was outward-looking and, just as importantly, to begin work on restructuring itself to become a truly open system. The committee did not find it particularly difficult to engage with the working hypothesis. This was, perhaps, because it gave concrete expression to what the committee already knew at an unconscious level—that it could no longer continue to respond in the same way to the increasing demands of current users.

CENTRAL ISSUES ARISING FROM THE FEEDBACK

The steering group created a process of analysis for itself which went from an initial stage of feeling almost overwhelmed by the mass of raw data from the interviews and the sense of chaos it presented, through a gradual distillation of central points, to the final articulation of the working hypothesis. The steering group decided to use a similar process for feedback to the committee, which would help them experience some of this diagnostic task. This was achieved by inviting them to respond to the data in the same step-by-step way as the steering group had done when doing their analysis and gradually clarifying and distilling the central issues for themselves.

Four central issues arose from the self-evaluation:

1. The organization needed to clarify its primary task in relation to community development. This had to be done in consultation with the local health authority. It could find at the end of this process that its primary task was not directly about social change but about individual and group development. This still necessitated its development as an open system if it was to target all those who might benefit from such a process.

2. Linked to this was the clear recognition that the Center was a first-stage center, offering people in the area a first step in moving out of their isolation and toward greater self-confidence. The Center could develop and assign some of its resources to second-stage development but only in proportion to its catering adequately for first-stage participants. By moving people on, the Center could continue to sell itself to the many people in the community who had not yet taken that first step.

Related to this was the need to build a culture or ethos of development beyond the Center. There was work to be done forging strong links with other resources in the area where people could choose to continue their development or where they could become involved in pursuing community agendas. This latter possibility related more closely to the agenda of social change of community development.

3. It was evident that the lack of adequate management structures contributed to the continuing confusion about the primary task, to the system having become closed, and to confusion about who was responsible for what.

4. The role of project leader would be affected significantly by any changes that might be made, and this would need to be worked through in a comprehensive way.

c⊗∽ﾟ

INSTRUCTIONS AND QUESTIONS

1. The BCRC case focuses on the concepts of "open" versus "closed" systems. Discuss the theme that "success can lead to failure," as it relates to the movement from open to closed in the BCRC.

2. The distinction between open and closed systems has a long history in the management sciences. Review that history, conveniently starting with sources such as the seminal 1964 book by Kahn and his associates, *Organizational Stress* (New York: John Wiley & Sons, Inc.).

3. A first stage in BCRC's evolution can be seen as grasping the complexity of the organization's context—social, historical, cultural, and economic. List the major factors or forces in this heightened complexity.

4. Does the concept of open vs. closed systems help you to understand the fates of other voluntary or third-sector organizations? Choose an exemplar in which you have an interest, such as the Young Men's Christian Association or the March of Dimes.

5. One can speak of BCRC as having reached a first phase or stage. What are your ideas and hunches about a second phase or stage? What would be needed to help BCRC move toward that second phase or stage?

References

Bion, W.R. (1969). *Experiences in groups.* New York: Routledge.

Block, P. (1981). *Flawless consulting.* San Diego, CA: University Associates Inc.

Czander, W. (1993). *The psychodynamics of work and organizations.* New York: Guilford Press.

Hirschorn, L. (1988). *The workplace within.* Cambridge, MA: MIT Press.

Holti, R. (1994a). *Summary of open systems concepts.* London: Tavistock Institute Advanced Organization Consultation Programme.

Holti, R. (1994b). *Under and over bounded systems.* London: Tavistock Institute Advanced Organization Consultation Programme.

Kahn, R.L., Wolfe, D.M., Quinn, R.P., Snoek, J.D., and Rosenthal, R.A. (1964). *Organizational stress: Studies in role conflict and ambiguity.* New York: John Wiley & Sons, Inc.

Menzies, I. (1975). Organization as a defense against anxiety. In A.D. Coleman & W.H. Bexton (Eds.), *A group relations reader.* New York: AK Rice Institute.

Miller, E. (1993). *From dependency to autonomy.* London: Free Association Books.

Miller, E. (1995). Dialogue with client systems: Use of the "working note" in organizational consultancy. *Journal of Managerial Psychology.* Special issue on action science and organizational research (ed. D. Coghlan), vol. 10 (6): 27–30.

Mintzberg, H. (1979). *The structuring of organizations.* New York: John Wiley & Sons.

Schein, E.H. (1987). *Process consultation,* vol. 2. Reading, MA: Addison-Wesley.

29

Moving Toward the Future

Many organizations in business, government, and the third sector are trying to develop approaches to planned change. Organizational environments are changing; hence, structures, policies, and missions have to adapt if the organization is to avoid being marginalized or even swept away.

The broad models guiding such efforts often have clear similarities. For example, they typically direct attention at the following factors:

- **what is**—i.e., the present state of an organization, perhaps describing it in terms of SWOT: Strengths, Weaknesses, Opportunities, and Threats;
- **what was**—the past state of an organization—trends, reasons for specific features of the present state, perspective on what things have been considered undoable;
- **what should be**—the features of the future desired or ideal condition;
- **how to get there**—the transition strategy and action plan for getting from the present state to the desired condition.

INSTRUCTIONS AND QUESTIONS

1. In outline form, use the above approach to analyze a third-sector organization of your choice. You may focus on a target organization in this casebook, one with which you have first-hand experience, or one requiring library visits to get enough information to proceed.
2. Consult some of the technical literature for guidance on enriching your approach. You might consult Beckhard and Harris, 1987; Weisbord, 1995; or similar sources, for this second go-around.

References

Beckhard, R., and Harris, R.T. (1987). *Organizational transitions.* Reading, MA: Addison-Wesley.

Weisbord, M.R. (1995). *Future search: An action guide to finding common ground in organizations and communities.* San Francisco, CA: Berrett-Koehler.

30

Putting the Pieces in Place

You are the Assistant Director of a large chapter of the American Red Cross. The Executive Director expects you to coordinate the chapter's day-to-day operations and lead the implementation of the new Performance Tracking System (PTS). PTS is the pet project of the chapter's Human Resources director who has been in place six months since arriving with the Executive Director from another chapter. She hit the ground running by introducing PTS to the chapter during the first month.

You have worked hard to integrate PTS into the management and personnel structure of the chapter's staff, but you felt some resistance from several of your division directors. PTS requires input and buy-in from each division, particularly in the goal-setting stage. Division directors are charged with developing "stretch" goals against which they and their employees will be measured. Top management formally signs-off on the selection of goals, and requires that they fit within national standards. Failure to accomplish these goals will reflect poorly on division directors. Your division directors are, however, accustomed to a more informal operation which has served them well for some time. After all, your chapter has been recognized as an outstanding organization by the National Red Cross. There's no arguing with success! Still, you want to serve your director and be a loyal employee. You want to cooperate with the Human Resources Director, even though she can be a bit stubborn and unbending at times.

PTS appears to be a good management tool that combines elements of the personnel function with accountability and wise use of resources. It is complex and has taken a lot of training to inform and convince key personnel to implement it. Of particular concern is the Director of Health and Safety Services. José is one of your best friends and has been extremely supportive of your work as Assistant Director. You are the first woman to be promoted to such a high position in this 200-employee organization. He has provided wise counsel during the past year since you took the post. Recently, he has been voicing his concerns about the workability of PTS, not just to you but to some of the other division directors. Not only are you worried that his opposition may severely damage your plan to fully implement PTS, you are concerned about him personally and his future in the organization. Specifically, José complained that

1. PTS was "rammed down the throats" of the staff without their being asked for input;
2. PTS is autocratic and depends on top-down direction and communication;
3. PTS is predicated on the premise that performance appraisal and management can be combined in one system;
4. PTS depends too much on external motivational strategies, rather than on self-discipline, intrinsic motivation, and personal initiative.

In the first round of division and personal goal-setting, José presented you with a half-page list of five objectives which he says are all he needs to write down. Missing are details related to time frame, direction of personnel within his division, and plans to work with other division directors. Further, he is convinced that the Executive Director and the Human Resources Director are having an affair. "After all," he said to you at lunch today, "they arrive together and go to lunch together nearly every day. Everybody knows they're sleeping together, and nobody can take their leadership seriously." You have wondered about that relationship, as well, but figured it was none of your business.

Beyond these particular worries, you are concerned with several more basic issues related to PTS. First, despite the apparent link between performance and reward, PTS seems to stress conformity of personal goals with a predetermined organizational mission. Second, the system appears to emphasize productivity over the original spirit of service that characterizes the Red Cross. Third, key chapter personnel are not keen on merit-based salary increases. They argue that such a system pits each of them against the others. Finally, you sense the absence of good communication among the division directors on goal-setting and follow-through.

You want to act quickly and positively to save PTS, particularly since the Executive Director has expressed his concern about its effectiveness. You are worried that if you design the wrong strategy, the whole program could blow up, causing serious morale problems.

INSTRUCTIONS AND QUESTIONS

1. What should you do first?
2. Develop a detailed action plan.

31

Knowing Why Makes the What and the How Straightforward

Michael O'Neill* directs forceful attention toward the numerous "ethical dimensions of the role of the manager in nonprofit organizations," and his conclusions demand careful consideration. His article takes what he calls "the still-radical position that ethics is a necessary and powerful aspect of organizational life."

Indeed, O'Neill also proposes that ethics is "the most important part" of executive responsibility and that this is true regardless of the type of organization that the executive calls home. O'Neill explains, "Ethics is primarily about what human persons do as individuals, but because of the enormous influence of formal organizations in our daily lives, increasing attention has been given to the ethical dimensions of organizations."

O'Neill asserts that his basic message has been honored only infrequently. Simply, he emphasizes that the demand for ethical administration far exceeds the supply: "Nearly all of this attention, unfortunately, has been extrinsic, negative, and scandal-driven, as if the only role of ethics were to prevent future Watergates and episodes of insider trading."

---

* Michael O'Neill, "Ethical Dimensions of Nonprofit Administration," *Nonprofit Management & Leadership*, 3 (Winter 1992): 199–213.

Consequently, it comes as no surprise that O'Neill urges special attention to nonprofit management, which combines a relevance to ethical issues with a lack of attention to them. He explains: "It is somewhat startling, not to say shocking, to see the extensive and often high-quality work that has gone into business and government ethics and then find virtually nothing on nonprofit ethics in general, though there has been some attention to specialized fields such as hospital administration and social service administration…there are historical reasons for this [shortfall]…primarily, the strong ethical traditions in the professions that make up much of the nonprofit sector, as well as the possible feeling that the sector that does good needn't worry about being good."

O'Neill (esp. p. 203) views the following dimensions as being of special relevance to nonprofit organizations, and he argues that NPOs successfully play their central roles to the degree that they give effective attention to each of these tasks:

- developing, shaping, and articulating values relevant not only to the nonprofit organization but also to numerous stakeholders as well as to the broader society;
- motivating and managing workers with mixed, and often-minimal, reliance on economic incentives;
- managing organizations that have large components of "professional workers" such as educational settings, hospitals, research organizations, and the like;
- managing organizations whose services cannot be monitored or evaluated well, or at least easily, by clients: day care centers, nursing homes, mental health services, and so on;
- managing organizations that have indistinct or unclear bottom-lines, both political and financial.

INSTRUCTIONS AND QUESTIONS

1. Accept O'Neill's challenge and develop a memo concerning ethics in nonprofits. Address this memo to the board of some NPO or voluntary agency you have in mind.

2. To add a bit of spice, now adopt one of the following two roles as writer: (a) the chief executive officer of the target NPO or voluntary agency; or (b) an "ethical resistor," or "whistleblower" concerned about the target NPO or voluntary agency.

32

Big John Changes Careers

You, "Big John" Frazier, are in the soup—big time. Today—April 28, 1997—will be your first day in your new job as Executive Director of Foundation X. X's mission is to variously help urban underprivileged children "from the cradle to graduate school," in the jocular way the insiders put it.

Less than a year ago, you were an offensive tackle for the pro football team housed in the city where Foundation X maintains its headquarters. As if in a continuous set of flashes, life moved on. There was that sickening snap in your left knee during the 1995 season, the long days of hoping that ended in an inability to perform in the fall 1996 football campaign, your retirement in early 1997, and then a long vacation. Shortly, and unexpectedly, after the retirement you were appointed Executive Director of Foundation X, to start just after that long-awaited vacation was over.

Your first media appearance would be on April 30, which when scheduled seemed very far away. Your wife, Amy, had her heart so set on that vacation that it became the only real deal-breaker. The board preferred an early start, but they were willing to wait those 90 days or so. You were delighted about the job: it fell in your lap, and the timing seemed just right. You could build up your knowledge base about volunteers and Foundation X at your leisure, and then ease into the job while the roar of the football crowd was still in your ears. You had done some volunteer work for Foundation X, in fact, and that is why you seemed to the board a natural candidate for the job. Many remembered an advertising campaign that featured you in full football gear, Foundation X's logo on your big chest, handing off the ball to a wide-eyed youngster. The tag-line for the campaign was a great one, and was well received: *"Big John can give you the ball, but only you can score!"* Of course, the ball also carried out the ad theme with a Foundation X label on the pigskin. Just give your clients the "ball" of Foundation X programs, and watch them go!

This campaign overstated matters in several regards. In reality, your knowledge of the Foundation was superficial, but people had begun referring to you as the X-man. But so much the better for your new career. It didn't seem to matter that the ad campaign suggested you were a quarterback, while you had been an offensive tackle. But that's show business! You luxuriated in your vacation and didn't do much to prepare for the X job.

Your expectations for a leisurely entrance into Foundation X recently dissolved. Major politicos, including President Clinton and former President Bush, began to see volunteerism as a major replacement for public services and programs now being axed. A potential president, General Colin Powell, will kick off a major volunteerism campaign on April 27 in Philadelphia, which has been getting the big build-up.

You would have known about this massing of wills even if you had not been attentive to the media. The board of Foundation X began whispering in your ear: Where do you stand on this "new volunteerism"? The whispers grew more like roars before your first day in office.

You won't be able to duck the scheduled major show-and-tell program on April 30. You, Big John Frazier, 6 feet 8 inches of ex-pro offensive tackle, are clearly going to be in another big game. You hoped you would be a better executive director than you were a footballer, where you got more publicity than statistics. You were a darling of the media as a pro, and you hope that will help until you get in the Foundation X rhythm.

But the bold fact is that you have not done enough preparation. Thus, your vacation extended beyond initial expectations; and then your flight back was delayed by mechanical problems on your return from the over-extended recreation period. And, bluntly, you had done only a little preparation—mostly, assembled a few clipping and notes in a single file folder labeled "The New Volunteerism" and made a brief side-trip to Washington, D.C.

So you have been much in the recent news; many stakeholders have raised their expectations about April 30; and you now sit at your desk at home, shaking out the pitiful contents of the file on new volunteerism that should be thick, but is not. In the early-morning hours of April 28, you are trying to review the file before leaving for work a bit later.

Exhibit 32-1.   Scraps of Notes and News Snippets in "New Volunteerism" File

---

Entry 1. John to Self (January 3)
What is really going on in this post-election attention to volunteerism, with Bush and Clinton joining forces?! Powell the top man, even though a potential presidential nominee in 2000?

Entry 2. John to Self (January 9)
The "New Volunteerism" will include major cross-currents. Will business corporations and the military be new major providers of volunteers? And what does that imply for "volunteerism"? Some talk even of payment for "volunteers." What does this imply for our real volunteers? What of contributions?

Entry 3. Questions, Questions (February 15–20)
What of the estimate by *Independent Sector* that there are 93 million American volunteers? Everybody seems to quote that number, e.g., Newt. If that number is correct, how come volunteers in Foundation X seem to be harder to find and keep? And if that number is correct, how can we get more of them for our share? Are corporations paying volunteers?

Entry 4. John for "New Volunteerism" File (March 1)
The "Summit for America's Future" seems like a solid go. My Board getting real interested. Are the pols really serious or is this just another hidden-ball trick?

Entry 5. Board Member to John C—e-mail (March 3)
We really need a strong statement from you, John, especially with the Summit coming up. We need to enlarge our base of support. We know you can do it, but we need to avoid the focus being shifted away from us!

Entry 6. John to Self (March 19)
My gosh. My short trip to D.C. really impressed. Everybody—liberal, conservative, and libertarian—sees a bigger role for volunteers and a smaller role for government. That train has already left the station! And I don't get the sense that Foundation X is on-board, or ought to be!

Entry 7. RE: "The Summit," *US News and World Report,* March 24, p. 9
News is starting to surface. Powell's "doctrine" is to apply military lessons to kids like ours! Is that our future? How do you apply "superior power" to the problems of poverty? And who defines the limited priorities for domestic problems?

Entry 8. RE: "The NV." *USA Today,* April 22, 1997, pp. 1–2
Omigosh! Volunteerism is first-page stuff along with women's athletics. *USA Today* reports on getting corporate muscle behind volunteerism. Will business millions be spent to pay volunteers? Where will those dollars really come from? What factors encourage the apparent buy-in by business? Somebody seems to have turned on the juice for Bush's "thousand points of light"?

Entry 9. "Do do-gooders do much good?" *US News and World Report,* April 28, p. 26 and 6 or 7 pages more.
A powerhouse piece! Why don't I just read this April 30?

* If there are really so many volunteers, why are our cities so much worse off?
* Is "real volunteerism" inherently localized, which means that the well-off help those most like themselves?
* Two working parents...?
* Need to get better at preparing/training volunteers to do tough jobs, at matching volunteers to person being helped.
* Are we loaded with recreational volunteers?

Entry 10. Where can I get more straight stuff about Clinton's Corporation for National Service?

Entry 11. John → Volunteerism File (April 27)
The "Summit" seems serious. Big numbers seem to have been pledged, by business and (if less so) by government. See Clinton's comments, Powell's.

* My fax is hot from notes from the Board! Maybe I should be happy that my e-mail seems to have crashed...
* And here comes the 30th! What looked like a nice, easy schedule has turned into a killer.

Entry 12. John → myself (April 28)
Well, "the Summit" seems a big hit. National Public Radio told me this morning that the occasion was a "media frenzy." Expectations for my launch are high and growing higher.

Looks like I'm in a big game without a real warm-up!

INSTRUCTIONS AND QUESTIONS

1. Begin preparing a list of "talking points" that you will emphasize in a speech and in a Q & A session to follow, based on the contents of your "New Volunteerism" file.

2. Detail any sources of information that will help you flesh out the initial list.

33

The Midvalley Recreation Department

The Midvalley Recreation Department serves a population that was formerly predominantly white, middle-class, and homogenous. In the past few years, however, the municipality has experienced significant demographic changes. It has seen tremendous growth in immigration, especially from eastern Asia and, to some extent, central Europe. One regularly hears many different languages spoken around town, and in general, the area seems less prosperous.

The Recreation Department Director is aware of these changes and others. Demand on the Department for more recreational leagues and facilities has increased dramatically over the past few years. Unfortunately, at some youth league games, ethnic and racial tensions have spilled over into problems on the field, such as abusive language, poor sportsmanship, and even fighting, and off the field with crowd control.

Earlier this year, the Recreation Department held a public meeting to assess the role of the Department in attending to the needs of the community. Residents urged the Recreation Department to consider providing new services and programs, including classes in sportsmanship and interracial understanding for all participants in recreational activities; improved crowd control and security at youth league games; a public address system to be used at championship events; additional athletic fields; lights for one athletic field; overhaul of the ice arena; more attention to girls' sports; and the provision of snacks for sale at youth league games.

Like many other public and nonprofit institutions, funding for the municipality of Midvalley has been cut back. At the present time, it is not possible to hire additional paid staff members for the Recreation Department, and any new programs or activities will require additional resources. Paid staff say that they already need more help in handling routine duties, such as laying out boundary lines on the athletic fields and keeping track of athletic equipment. At the public meeting, the Recreation Department Director pointed out these realities to residents. In return, some of them expressed an interest in forming an auxiliary fund-raising group—if the Recreation Department would take the lead in organizing it.

BACKGROUND ON THE MIDVALLEY RECREATION DEPARTMENT VOLUNTEER PROGRAM

Until recently, the tasks of locating, recruiting, and retaining volunteers have not been difficult for the Midvalley Recreation Department. The volunteer corps has consisted almost entirely of middle-aged, white males, who served as unpaid coaches and referees for the youth leagues. Many of these volunteers have left the area as their children have matured.

The departing head of the volunteer program was unpaid and had no training in the field of volunteer administration. He said that he was resigning because the job had grown too frustrating (actually, he used somewhat stronger language). In particular, he said that attracting and keeping good volunteers had become very difficult: "They like sports, but they get tired of doing the same old jobs." Paid staff had added to his frustrations. Some had criticized volunteers in public. They complained to him about volunteers "not showing up," and "quitting without notice"; a few volunteers wanted to "manage things" or "take over." He felt that "Morale among paid employees is poor. They have too much to do, and they resent working with this new type of abusive kid we seem to be getting. To some of these employees, right now, volunteers seem to be just one more problem."

INSTRUCTIONS AND QUESTIONS

The head of the Volunteers Corps for the Midvalley Recreation Department has resigned. You are a new member of a selection committee choosing a replacement who will act as spokesperson for the Corps. The selection committee also will help the chosen candidate to assume responsibility for the volunteer program.

1. What needs to be done to strengthen the volunteer program and assist the Recreation Department in serving the community?
2. Rank the needs identified in order of priority.
3. Recommend action steps for each priority.

34

Three Go-Arounds Toward Assessing a Nonprofit

The literature in the field of organizational development has for decades emphasized continuous self-assessment of all organizations, and the basic reasons seem clear enough. Excellence will come only from concerted and consistent efforts to deal with the basic questions of why and how organization members go about their business. Thus, people in organizations need to be self-reflective and self-reflexive; to seek to gain insight on what they are doing, and to act on that insight to do better. The time-frame is continuous, rather than episodic.

The rationale for this advice has been extended in forceful and useful ways to nonprofits. The Peter F. Drucker Foundation for Nonprofit Management (1993) provides a format for self-assessment that is flexible enough to be acted on in short time periods. Thus, more or less continuously, one can use the Foundation approach to reflect on one's own experiences in a nonprofit. Relatedly, the Foundation approach can be used in more formal ways by collectives: a work team, representatives of a department, or a planning team for an entire nonprofit. Typically, these collective efforts can be scheduled at regular intervals, say, yearly. But there is no reason why even such collectives cannot be quickly set in motion as contingencies recommend or require.

TWO INITIAL STEPS, SMALL VARIETY

The reader can take a first step to checking out the usefulness of the Drucker Foundation approach by using the broad format of the following five key questions developed by Drucker himself (1993):

1. Why is the targeted nonprofit in business? What are its missions?
2. Who are the customers of the targeted nonprofit?
3. What do the customers need or want that the target nonprofit might provide?
4. How successful has the targeted nonprofit been in providing the desired services to its customers?
5. How does the targeted nonprofit plan to better provide such services? What improvements can be made in that plan?

INSTRUCTIONS AND QUESTIONS

1. Focus on a particular nonprofit—either one in which you are a member, or a nonprofit you would like to learn about through library research or interviews with the agency's employees and volunteers.
2. Try to answer Drucker's five key questions for the selected nonprofit. Different readers no doubt will have different interpretations of Drucker's questions; nevertheless, given the general character of the key questions, do they help the reader gain perspective on the targeted nonprofit?
3. (Optional) Provide a detailed analysis of the targeted nonprofit, again using the five key Drucker questions, but this time in more detailed ways. You need not develop more detailed versions of Drucker's questions on your own. Drucker (1994) has provided a detailed elaboration of the five key questions, along with a workbook that can be purchased to facilitate analysis, or at least consulted to give the reader a comprehensive sense of what Drucker has in mind.

References

Drucker, P.F. (1994). *The five most important questions you will ever ask about your nonprofit organization*. San Francisco: Jossey-Bass.

The Peter F. Drucker Foundation for Nonprofit Management (1993). *How to assess your nonprofit organization*. (User Guide for Boards, Staff, Volunteers, and Facilitators). San Francisco: Jossey-Bass.

35

Dual Roles and Conflict in Voluntary Organizations*

In voluntary organizations, particularly information or crisis agencies, volunteer members are found serving as both service providers and members of the board of directors. Such dual roles may lead to problems for both the organization and for the individual. For the organization there may be problems about the supervisory role and for the individual role confusion and conflict. This article reports on a study of two agencies that experienced conflict and confusion in this regard. It draws on domain theory as a resource for organization development consultants who may have to deal with such problems in their work in voluntary organizations.

INTRODUCTION

Organization development consultants who work with both for-profit and not-for-profit organizations find that they are similar in many respects. Volunteers, however, are found almost exclusively in nonprofit or voluntary organizations and offer a unique set

*Reprinted with permission from Candace Widmer, "Volunteers with the Dual Roles of Provider and Board Member," *Organization Development Journal*, 14 (Fall 1996): 54–60.

of challenges to consultants helping these organizations manage change. Volunteers are especially important to human service organizations and in some cases carry out the "real work," the mission, of the agency. This seems to be particularly true of crisis and information services. Volunteers in these organizations provide information, advocacy, crisis intervention, counseling, and/or accompaniment services to agency clients. They are often the primary, and sometimes the sole, service providers.

Information and crisis agencies frequently have volunteers who serve as service providers and volunteers who serve on the board of directors. In some cases, the same individual serves in both of these roles. In my research on the boards of directors of human service organizations (Widmer, 1985, 1987, 1993) as well as in my consulting with nonprofit agencies, every organization in which the same individuals serve as both service providers and board members reported "problems" arising from this arrangement. After experiencing these problems first-hand as a consultant with a crisis agency, I undertook the study described here.

Problems in the management of volunteers are not unexpected and have been reported by many others. Mason, in writing about the management implications of volunteer staff, provided the following example:

> For instance, Ann, the college-educated wife of a $100,000-a-year business and civic leader, might volunteer to be part of a group that will canvass a neighborhood. How accurately they identify the number of senior adults will influence the job security of a 24-year-old social worker named John. When wearing another hat, Ann sits on the organization's board. Will she see her canvassing job as an assignment that properly requires her to work under the supervision of John? Will he make accommodations for her status in another relationship? What if a grant from the company of Ann's husband is paying for the whole project? What if she takes an out-of-town trip at a crucial time without notification? Does John replace her, do the job himself, or expect her to double up when she returns? (Mason, 1984, p. 61).

Mason focuses on monitoring volunteer performance and on managing status inconsistencies, but some of the problems he describes, and I have found, arise because of role conflict or role confusion. "Ann" is both a volunteer and a board member. She has two roles in this organization.

Role theorists suggest that problematic interactions may arise when a role actor cannot choose a role because he or she either doesn't know an appropriate role or knows several and doesn't know which to choose, when there is a lack of consensus about a role between the role actor and others, or when there are incompatibilities among or within roles. Any or all of these situations may arise for volunteers in human service agencies. Role conflict—conflict that arises when an individual receives incompatible messages regarding appropriate role behavior—and role ambiguity—uncertainty as to appropriate role behaviors—seem particularly likely to occur in organizations when volunteers play more than one role. (For a more complete discussion of role theory see Biddle and Thomas, 1966; Heiss, 1981, p. 117; Katz and Kahn, 1978; Sell, Brief, and Schuler, 1981; and Turner, 1978, pp. 350–351. For a more complete discussion of role conflict in boards of directors of nonprofit human service agencies, see Widmer, 1993.)

Role conflict is undesirable not only because it makes people uncomfortable (and makes volunteers leave), but also because it makes organizations ineffective. Role conflict leads to dissatisfaction, less confidence in the organization, lower productivity, poor performance, poor goal achievement, poor interpersonal relationships, tension, and stress (Baron, 1986, p. 209; Hellriegel, Slocum, and Woodman, 1983, pp. 246–249, 474–475; Merz, 1984; and Sell et al., 1981).

Why does having volunteers who are both service providers and board members create problems? Can organization development consultants help manage these tensions? Is role conflict inevitable in agencies with such an arrangement? Or are problems due simply to confusion in the minds of the role actors? Can organizations with volunteer service providers/board members eliminate or reduce conflict and/or confusion? Or must organizations either change their structure or simply learn to live with their problems? These were the questions I asked myself and which I carried into the research reported here. I wanted to understand the "problems" agencies were reporting and, if possible, to help agencies deal effectively with them.

METHODS

The subjects for this study were two not-for-profit human service agencies in New York State's Southern Tier. Both agencies provide counseling, advocacy, and/or information services to clients who call or come into the agency. Counseling/advocacy/information is provided to clients of these agencies primarily by unpaid volunteers, who are supervised by paid staff members. In both agencies some of the volunteer service providers are also members of the agency board of directors.

Interviews were conducted with executive directors, staff members, board presidents, volunteer service providers, and board members of the agencies. The interview instrument used included both open and closed questions and was modified as the research progressed. Most interviews took place in person; a few were carried out by telephone. Interviews were conducted with both individuals and groups. In all, 30 individuals were interviewed.

RESULTS AND DISCUSSION

As preliminary findings had suggested, both organizations reported problems as a result of having volunteer service providers who were also board members. The problems reported, which were not identical, can be characterized as follows:

- conflict and/or confusion about supervisory roles;
- conflict and/or confusion about the role of the board; or
- conflict and/or confusion about the role of board member.

Each of these problems areas is discussed below.

Conflict and/or Confusion About Supervisory Roles

Both agencies reported that they had, either currently or in the past, experienced problems with the supervision of volunteers. Some of these problems arose because volunteers are more difficult to supervise than paid staff members, in part because supervisors often have less control over the incentives of volunteers.

Other problems with supervision arose because supervisors sometimes felt uncomfortable criticizing or evaluating a volunteer because of the volunteer's status. This problem, like the situation described by Mason, is likely to occur whenever a staff member perceives a volunteer to have superior status due to age, race, sex, class, eduction, or other status characteristics. It also occurs when a volunteer is perceived as higher in status because of his or her position as a board member or board officer. When status incongruity exists, role conflict and ambiguity are intensified. In this study, the organization with the more clearly defined supervisory structure had less discomfort around issues of status and position. This organization, which had previously experienced problems with volunteer supervision, reported that their most recent volunteer coordinator was viewed as "legitimate" because of his social work training and had few difficulties with the supervision of volunteers.

Other supervisory problems arose specifically because of the dual roles of the volunteer service provider/board members. One agency's members talked about the supervisory process "being like a circle" and "chasing its tail." Members reported that the volunteer service providers were supervised by a volunteer coordinator who was supervised by the executive director who was supervised by the board including volunteer service providers. This arrangement was perceived as threatening, particularly by agency staff members who felt that the board had intervened and might continue to intervene in their work. Unwanted intervention had occurred most often when there was no other avenue, except through the volunteer service provider/board members, through which volunteer service providers could express dissatisfaction with conditions.

The other agency also reported problems with supervision due to the dual role of volunteers. "It blurs the hierarchy of board, staff, volunteers," one board member reported. "Staff members sometimes get by-passed in information and discussion."

Conflict and/or Confusion About the Role of the Board

Most writers on boards suggest that staff, executive director, and board roles should be clearly differentiated. Indeed, in previous studies (Widmer, 1993), organizations in which the role of the board was least clearly defined had the most conflict and confusion. But, although most researchers and practitioners agree that policy making is the role of the board and implementation is the role of the staff, what is seen as implementation in one agency may be seen as policy making in another. In agencies where volunteers serve as both service providers and board members, conflict and confusion over the board's and the staff's responsibility is exacerbated. Those who are implementing policy are also making it. In addition, volunteer service provider/board members know the intimate details of the agency and bring this knowledge to the policy-making process. Their knowledge of the agency may help the board understand the implications of the policy choices before them, but it also enables the board to stray into areas of the agency's operations which are usually unknown to and thus untouched by the board.

Conflict and/or Confusion About the Role of Board Member

The agencies in this study also reported conflict and confusion around the role of board member. Volunteer service provider/board members bring their experience to the board. The boards of these agencies have chosen to include volunteer service provider/board members on their boards for this reason, but there is often disagreement about the appropriate role of such board members. Conflict centers on whether the volunteer service provider/board members should be "representatives" of the volunteer service providers or "trustees" of the agency like (at least theoretically) other board members.

Most of the volunteer service provider/board members I interviewed felt that their primary role on the board was that of "representative," "reporter," "spokesperson," or "liaison." A few were unsure about their role. Most of the other volunteer service providers seemed to feel that the volunteer service provider/board members should vote in accord with the opinions of the service providers. Most of the other board members and staff members seemed to feel that the volunteer service provider/board members should play their role more like that of the other board members. The net effect was twofold: not only did agency members disagree on the role to be played, but the difference between the way volunteer service provider/board members and other board members played their roles created two categories of board members. This distinction was enhanced by differences in election procedures and length of term between the two types of board members.

Volunteer service provider/board members had different perspectives as well as different roles. Volunteer service provider/board members, who, as one board member put it, "live the details" of implementation, were more likely to focus on these details than were other board members who lack this perspective. In addition, volunteer service provider/board members were often truly knowledgeable about only the service delivery part of the organization. Volunteer service provider/board members also seemed to differ from other board members in the amount of board experience they had. For some at least, board membership was a "pay back for volunteering as a service provider." Many had not served on a board before.

Although these differences were sometimes divisive, most volunteer service provider/board members were clear: they saw themselves first and foremost as service providers. The conviction with which the volunteer service provider/board members held this identity made it difficult for them to understand why staff members might see them as powerful and somewhat intimidating service provider/board member hybrids. Indeed, volunteer service provider/board members often assured staff members that they were service providers and not policy makers or supervisors.

Some volunteer service provider/board members, however, adopted a broader perspective on board issues and spoke less as service providers and more like other board members. Some left their role as service provider and became "regular" members of the board. In at least one instance, this created additional tension between the volunteer service providers and the board.

The problems reported by the agencies in this study differed in detail, and not all can be reported here, both because further detail is unnecessary and because detail may violate the confidentiality of those interviewed. But all of the problems reported can be categorized as above—as disagreement and/or uncertainty about the proper role of the board and the appropriate roles of volunteers and staff members. In addition, it is interesting to note that when asked if the problems experienced by their agency represented conflict or confusion, respondents consistently answered "both."

CONCLUSION

Although the problems reported by the two agencies were similar, they were not identical. One board had found solutions to some of the problems experienced by the other. Both had traded in old problems for new ones. Both of these agencies were working hard to address their problems, but both continued to experience problems that seemed to stem from having volunteer service providers who are also board members. Why does this particular structure result in conflict *and* confusion? Can organizations reach agreement about appropriate roles, resolve ambiguity, and eliminate such problems?

Certainly conflict can be reduced. The agencies in this study had done so. Openly addressing concerns about supervision had reduced conflict. Providing clear channels for the expression of service provider concerns had reduced confusion. But the ubiquity and persistence of these problems suggest some kind of underlying and unresolvable conflict. The role conflict observed here may be the inevitable result of the dual roles played by volunteer service provider/board members, or there may be additional structural factors leading to the incompatibility of role expectations that role theory suggests leads to role conflict.

Domain Theory, developed by Kouzes and Mico (1979) in an attempt to explain their own observations as consultants to human service organizations, may help to explain the observed role conflict. Domain Theory suggests that human service agencies are made up of three domains: a service domain, a management domain, and a policy domain. The members of these domains not only have different roles, they have different identities, work modes, norms, and values. According to Domain Theory, this "create[s] natural conditions of disjunction and discordance" (Kouzes and Mico, 1979, p. 449).

According to this theory of conflicting domains, in the situation described above, service providers are part of the service domain and follow professional norms as counselors, even though they may be volunteers. Their primary duty is to provide quality service to their clients. Board members, on the other hand, are members of the policy domain. Members of the policy domain are loyal to the principle of equity and norms of fairness and impartiality. Their duty is to the agency and to the community. Conflict and confusion may be due not only to the dual roles played by the volunteer service provider/board members, but also, Domain Theory would suggest, to the location of these roles in different domains.

What can organizations and consultants do to manage role conflict? Organizations can change their structure, eliminate volunteer service provider/board members and lose the knowledge and experience they bring to board deliberations. Or they can live with their volunteer service provider/board members and the problems they bring and try to reduce the conflict and confusion whenever they can. Organization development consultants can help organizations explore the advantages and disadvantages of both alternatives and make an informed choice.

INSTRUCTIONS AND QUESTIONS

1. Does the picture of the role dynamics in the two focal organizations strike you as a realistic description of what goes on in voluntary organizations you know about or have read about? If you cannot decide about the representativeness of the case, how would you go about getting a better sense of what exists?

2. Visit a local voluntary organization and test by interviews and perhaps observation for role conflict of the kind described in this case.

References

Baron, R.A. (1986). *Behavior in organizations.* Boston: Allyn and Bacon.

Biddle, B.J., and Thomas, E.J. (1966). *Role theory: Concepts and research.* New York: John Wiley & Sons.

Heiss, J. (1981). Social roles. In M. Rosenberg and R.H. Turner (Eds.), *Social psychology: Sociological perspectives.* New York: Basic Books.

Hellriegel, D., Slocum, J.W., and Woodman, R.W. (1983). *Organizational behavior.* St. Paul, MN: West.

Katz, D., and Kahn, R.L. (1978). *The social psychology of organizations.* New York: John Wiley & Sons.

Kouzes, J.M., and Mico, P.R. (1979). Domain theory: An introduction to organizational behavior in human service organizations. *The Journal of Applied Behavioral Science, 15*(4): 449–469.

Mason, D.E. (1984). *Voluntary nonprofit enterprise management.* New York: Plenum.

Merz, C.S. (1984). *Conflict and frustration for school board members.* Paper presented at the Annual Meeting of the American Educational Research Association, New Orleans, April 1984.

Sell, M.V., Brief, A.P., and Schuler, R.S. (1981). Role conflict and role ambiguity: Integration of the literature and directions for future research. *Human Relations, 34*(1): 43–71.

Turner, Jonathan H. (1978). *The structure of sociological theory.* Homewood, IL: Dorsey.

Widmer, C. (1985). Why board members participate. *Journal of Voluntary Action Research, 14*(4): 8–23.

Widmer, C. (1987). Minority participation on boards of directors of human service agencies: Some evidence and suggestions. *Journal of Voluntary Action Research, 16*(4): 33–43.

Widmer, C. (1993). Role conflict, role ambiguity, and role overload on boards of directors of nonprofit human service organizations. *Nonprofit and Voluntary Sector Quarterly, 22*(4): 339–356.

Cases by Contributor*

*Some contributors prefer to remain anonymous.

Contributors to Series of Casebooks

Thomas E. Allen, Jr.
David B. Amick
Francis P. Anzelmi
Steven H. Appelbaum
Richard M. Ayres
Elaine Baker
J. Norman Baldwin
Darold T. Barnum
Raymond G. Beck
Wendell Broadwell
David S. Brown
Jeffrey L. Brudney
Thomas G. Butts
Bonnie L. Clark
Ross Clayton
David Coghlan
Robert W. Cole
Steve Condrey
Debbie Cutchin
J. Shannon Davis
Bryan Day
Gemma Donnelly-Cox
John Ellis
Marilyn Farley

Charles W. Fleming
Asa B. Foster, Jr.
Charles N. Fowler
Ronald Fraser
Steven B. Frates
Bruce Fusner
William C. Gaines
Vickie Gates
John Gehl
Horst B. Glatte
Margaret H. Golembiewski
Robert T. Golembiewski
Pati Gopal
Timothy J. Gorgg
George E. Hale
Meredith Anne Hart
Robert C. Helt
Patrick Henningan
Bob M. Inge
Robert G. Johnson
Gwendolyn L. Jones
Robert Kershaw
Jonathan Kleinwarks
Mark Kohntopp

Robert S. LaSala

Edward Anthony Lehan

Jeff T. Lewis

John Maples

Anthony R. Marchione

Albert R. Martin

David Mason

Richard Mays

Alan McClain

Francis P. McGee

Maureen M. McIntosh

Joseph A. Mitchell

Robin Mullin

Robert Murtagh

David O'Brien

Harry G. Perkins

Donald R. Peterson

Joyce Plotkin

Ernest Powell, Jr.

Dewey Price

Gerard J. Quinn

John H. Rheinscheld

Wilber C. Rich

Dorothy Jane Riggs

Matthews J. Robbins

Roby D. Robertson

Philip Rosenberg

Richard D. Schmitt

Bob Schultz

G. W. Sheldon

Gordon M. Sherman

Frank R. Shults

Lawrence L. Singer

David W. Sink

Patricia Somers

Jane Freeman Steagall

Eldon Steeves

Jerry G. Stevenson

Joe C. Strange

Kecia Thomas

Ronald E. Usher

Stuart Vexler

Jennifer A. Wade

Eugene W. Washington

Thomas L. Wheelen

Michael White

Candace Widmer

Steven C. Wilkins

Roger Williams

James Winship

CASES AND APPLICATIONS IN NONPROFIT MANAGEMENT
Edited by Janet Tilden
Production supervision by Kim Vander Steen
Cover design by Lesiak/Crampton Design, Park Ridge, Illinois
Composition by Point West, Inc., Carol Stream, Illinois
Paper, Finch Opaque
Printed and bound by McNaughton & Gunn, Saline, Michigan